HAPPY
ARE
YOU
WHO
AFFIRM

A book of reflections

HAPPY ARE YOU WHO AFFIRM

THOMAS A. KANE, PH.D., D.P.S.

AFFIRMATION BOOKS
WHITINSVILLE, MASSACHUSETTS

Published With Ecclesiastical Permission

First Edition
©1980 by House of Affirmation, Inc.

Acknowledgements

Excerpt from *A Sleep of Prisoners* by Christopher Fry reprinted by permission of Oxford University Press, Inc. Copyright © 1951, 1979 by Christopher Fry.

Library of Congress Cataloging in Publication Data
Kane, Thomas A. 1940-
  Happy are you who affirm.
1. Christian life—Catholic authors.
I. Title
BX2182.2.K32   248'4-82   80-26834
ISBN 0-89571-010-2

Printed by Mercantile Printing Company, Worcester, Massachusetts
United States of America

This book is dedicated to

BERNARD J. FLANAGAN
Bishop of Worcester

who teaches us how gentle
shepherding affirms

All income derived from the sale of this book is applied to providing care for clergy and religious suffering from emotional unrest.

AFFIRMATION BOOKS is an important part of the ministry of the House of Affirmation, International Therapeutic Center for Clergy and Religious, founded by Sr. Anna Polcino, S.C.M.M., M.D.

Illustration credits: Bonnie Ashe, p. 50; Sister Theresa Ramirez, S.S.M., p. 136; Sister Christine Soldenski, O.S.F., p. 148; Verna Stroeder, pp. 84, 120; Worcester Telegram and Gazette, p. 20.

Dark and cold we may be, but this
Is no winter now. The frozen misery
Of centuries breaks, cracks, begins to move,
The thunder is the thunder of the floes
The thaw, the flood, the upstart Spring.
Thank God our time is now when wrong
Comes up to face us everywhere,
Never to leave us till we take
The longest stride of soul men ever took.
Affairs are now soul size.
The enterprise
Is exploration into God.

Christopher Fry
A Sleep of Prisoners

CONTENTS

INTRODUCTION

Happy Are You Who Affirm is about life, its struggle and its beauty. This book does not have all the answers concerning our journey in life, but it does have some of them. The reader is invited to pause and consider the thoughts expressed herein. Hopefully, this book of reflections will inspire others to further written expressions of affirmation and to expressions in song and dance.

This book is about affirmation. I make no claims to having discovered a new theory of affirmation. Those who do make such claims often appear to lack any scientific or theological foundations on which to base them. I am indebted to the writings and scholarship of Martin Buber, and to the German Thomistic philosopher Josef Pieper. Buber and Pieper are the great names in philosophical and psychological thought concerning affirmation. Affirmation is basically gospel living, and though my psychotheological approach to this topic is original, certainly this approach is one of emphasis and explanation rather than discovery.

Affirmation is a gift which we give to another. We cannot give it to ourselves. In a certain sense, we cannot affirm ourselves. Affirmation is not just an intellectual assent; rather, it is the process which brings happiness to my life because of the people, for better and for worse, who have entered my life. Our model for affirmation is Jesus, who said: "Love one another as I have loved you" (John 13:34). Jesus is the one who gives us the gift, sends us on the journey, and encourages us, as incomplete people, with the fullness of his love and mercy.

This book draws upon the insights of both theology and psychology, and, in combining them, arrives at a psycho-theological approach. It reflects on the experience of many of the great truths of our Judeo-Christian tradition; it emphasizes that theological and scientific truths are essentially intermingled and mutually illuminating.

The first encounter with the term "psychotheological" could evoke the image of some new hybrid science with its own independent subject matter and means of inquiry. However, strictly speaking, psychotheology is not a science. It is rather an approach to life which draws on secular and religious sources of truth combined to better our response to the total human person as created, redeemed, and called by God in Christ Jesus. This view of the human person is an acknowledgment of the integration of the human and divine which already exists perfectly in Christ and which serves as the inspiring vision, the reassuring reality, the very way to the Father, shared by all Christians on the journey to their own hearts.

Primarily, integration of the human and divine must begin to take place within the heart of the human person. The open heart is the only soil in which the word of God and his grace can take root. God does not work in a vacuum nor does he say no to his own creation. Whatever helps us to find our true hearts and opens them to God in our life experience is good mental health at work. It is also God at work. The integration of the human and the divine that a psychotheological approach to the human person seeks is what Christ seeks.

There is also an integration of psychology and theology at a secondary level which guides us in our attempts to achieve the primary integration in our hearts. This union occurs at the level of knowledge and insight. It must be emphasized that such an integration does not blur the distinction between nature and grace, between the natural and the supernatural, between psychology and theology. Neither does it deny the palpable presence of God in many people who cannot achieve the primary integration of the human and divine. If anything, this union heightens our appreciation of both psychology and theology and prompts us to listen more respectfully to God speaking in them by honoring the noblest traditions of each science. The knowledge and insight gained by a dialogue between these areas of God's truth comes from the mutual highlighting of areas of human experience produced, in turn, by both theology and psychology. Each science, in its own way, provides an increased awareness, an illumination and unravelling of the human experience, in which God speaks and responds to his precious creation, leading especially to personal growth within a family or community setting.

A psychotheological approach to the problems of living is a source of nourishment for solutions to these problems. If society is to be healed and the identity of each individual is to be assured, there must be an increased awareness of the need for the integrated development of the physical, mental, and spiritual aspects of the whole person.

So many people deserve to be thanked here for encouraging and affirming me. Hopefully, I have thanked, by word and action, those who should know my appreciation. I must make special note of my foreign students who have taught me so many cross-cultural insights, particularly those from Canada, Ireland, England, France, Italy, India, Hong Kong, Nigeria, Iran, South Africa, Mexico, Nicaragua, and Australia. They came here to America to learn, but in many ways they were my teachers. Also, I wish to thank my bishop, to whom this book is dedicated. He is a wonderful and courageous man, forgiving and reconciling. I have received the healing touch of affirmation from him in a way I doubt he will fully recognize. I continue to appreciate the dedication of my secretary, Mrs. Terry Murphy, and my editor, Sister Marie Kraus, S.N.D.

I continue to be affirmed by and to remember with affection all residents and staff, present and former, of the House of Affirmation family here in America and in the United Kingdom.

Thomas A. Kane
Feast of Saint Anne
July 26, 1980

Chapter I

Happy Are You

Happiness is not in our circumstances, but in ourselves. It is not something we see, like a rainbow, or feel, like the heat of a fire. Happiness is something we are.

—John B. Sheerin

When I was a little boy, I learned from my mom and dad that "God made me to know him, love him, serve him, and be *happy* with him in this life and in the next." It seemed that God and my parents wanted the same thing for me—happiness. Thus, I grew up thinking that happiness is what life is all about. In fact, upon entering adulthood I learned that everything people do—their goals, aspirations, and dreams—revolves around happiness. Faith, love, religion, achievement, friendship, sex, recognition, vocation—everything that is important to us is a means to achieving happiness, and we do our best to change whatever interferes with that happiness.

As Americans, our Constitution guarantees us "life . . . liberty and the pursuit of happiness." The philosopher George Santayana wrote, "Happiness is the only sanction of life; where happiness fails, existence remains a mad, lamentable experiment." Saint Thomas Aquinas, whose teachings echo through the centuries, emphasized that "by nature, a person endowed with reason wishes to be happy and therefore cannot wish not to be happy!"

When is the last time you read anything about happiness? When is the last time you talked with somebody about happiness or heard a sermon, a lecture, or even participated in a good discussion about happiness? Was it on a television commercial that promised instant happiness if you used such and such toothpaste? Was the last time you considered happiness when you received the pay increase which would allow more things to be bought? Happiness posters abound these days. I saw one the other day which said, "Happiness is having a fuel-efficient car," and still another that stated, "Happiness is having it twice daily." I do not know what the it referred to, but I can imagine. A friend of mine wears a tee shirt that states, "Happiness is owning an English bulldog."

What is Happiness?

If we look at some American studies of attitudes, we find that most Americans are really happy people. The results of a *Psychology Today* questionnaire indicated that sixty percent of the respondents had been "moderately happy" or "very happy" in the last six months. A survey published by the popular family magazine *Good Housekeeping* reported even more happiness—seventy percent of the respondents stated that they had been "moderately happy" or "very happy" over the last six months.[1] There are other more scientific studies, I am sure, but I think it is valid to state generally that most Americans are happy. This is true despite the obvious fact that this country has been experiencing difficult times in the form of inflation, unemployment, political corruption, and general upset in values.

It has been my privileged position to travel and lecture extensively in many parts of the world. I must honestly report that what I observe, specifically true of Americans, I find generally true of most people in our world, some of whom live in political turmoil and unspeakable living conditions; namely, most people are indeed happy.

What makes people happy can vary considerably. The many elements that contribute to happiness can be divided into groups:

1. *The Social*—marriage, family, friends, children;
2. *The Economic*—job, income, standard of living, financial security;
3. *The Personal*—success, personal growth, physical and mental health, freedom, independence;
4. *The Spiritual*—leisure time for reflection, internal peace, faith, religion, belief in the absolute.

Happiness is Relationship

The complexity of human living certainly testifies that there is no simple recipe for producing happiness. However, the poets, songwriters, philosophers, and theologians, as well as the immediate authority of every living

---

1. Jonathan Freedman, *Happy People* (New York: Harcourt, Brace, Jovanovich, 1978), p. 36.

human being, point to one necessary ingredient—some kind of intimate relationship. Relationship is what life is all about: relationship with one's world, self, others, and God.

Christianity is all about relationship. Its essential teaching is that when persons are respectfully intimate with their lover, friend, neighbor, God, and world, the result is happiness "in this life and the next." In fact, so important is relationship in Christian theology that it teaches that the love relationship of Father for Son and Son for Father is so meaningful that this relationship results in a person— Love—whom we call the Holy Spirit.

Affirmation is all about relationship. As we progress in this book we will learn about affirmation and how, indeed, the *product* of affirmation is happiness. There are many elements related to happiness but it is impossible to list a set of requirements and state that these necessarily will bring about happiness. However, we do know that those who affirm and are affirmed are happy people. The affirmed person learns how to live life to the fullest, no matter what the life circumstances happen to be.

The happiness that is produced by affirmation is no quickly delivered accomplishment. It is produced by way of pilgrimage, a journey in life which involves birth, pain, growth, change, and peace. Let us go to the mountain of the beatitudes. There we look at the Lord, listen to his word, and absorb his "happy are you." Through the Good News that he speaks to us we can understand what the Lord expects of us here and now. He is our affirmer. He is the way, the truth, and the life.

Let us forget for a while all our daily cares so we can listen intently to the message of the Lord. Soon we will realize that there is room for the images of our daily lives in the clear air on the mountain of the beatitudes. For the Lord takes us infinitely seriously *just as we are*. He has a message for us which sheds light on our questions about life and happiness: "You are the light of the world" (Matt. 5:14).

The Beatitudes

How happy are the poor in spirit:
theirs is the kingdom of heaven.
Happy the gentle:
they shall have the earth for their heritage.
Happy those who mourn:
they shall be comforted.
Happy those who hunger and thirst for what is right:
they shall be satisfied.
Happy the merciful:
they shall have mercy shown them.
Happy the pure in heart:
they shall see God.
Happy the peacemakers:
they shall be called children of God.
Happy those who are persecuted in the cause of right:
theirs is the kingdom of heaven.

(Matt. 5:3-12)

Mother Teresa, of Calcutta, Nobel-prizewinning mission-ary, asked if she does not become discouraged in her work with the destitute and dying: "GOD HAS NOT CALLED ME TO BE SUCCESSFUL. HE HAS CALLED ME TO BE FAITHFUL."

Chapter II

Adult Living is Difficult Work

For us, there is only
the trying
The rest is not our
business.

—T. S. Eliot

Journeys are never easy. We grow tired travelling, we miss our connections, we find ourselves among strangers. But these drawbacks are more than balanced by the changing scenes we view, the new friends we make, the experiences through which we grow.

Why, then, do we expect the journey of life to be without pain or difficulties? For Christians, life is a special kind of journey, a pilgrimage. We begin at birth to travel toward the ultimate holy place, heaven. The purpose of a pilgrimage is not primarily enjoyment. Pilgrims concentrate on the spiritual purpose of their journey, not the convenience of their travel arrangements.

During the last few years numerous how-to books have been offered to the reading public: how to be happy, successful, popular—*instantly.* This is nonsense. There is no magic formula to make life easy. There is no quick cure for the problems we face in life and the weaknesses we find within ourselves. If we think that life should and can be always serene and easy, we are entertaining a naive childish fantasy.

Sloppy Miracle Talk

I want to make it clear that I do not promise you any such ideal living after you read this book. Anyone who promises either a quick miracle or a fast cure is theologically and clinically irresponsible. Miracles do happen, miracles of grace, but to promise them as a common occurrence is to promise something that cannot be guaranteed.

The mature person realizes that adult living is difficult work, that there is pain, tension, and anxiety in our days as well as happiness and peace. Because theology today emphasizes the Resurrection, we must not forget that Christ suffered the Gethsemane experience and travelled the Way of the Cross.

Love and Pain

Shortly before the Somoza regime fell in Nicaragua, I was invited to give a workshop for a group of American Franciscans, many of whom had spent years in the tropical jungle with the Indians. Although I was invited to teach there, I soon realized I was the student. I learned much about the living Gospel from these priests and the people they served. One day, I was walking through a village in which there was poverty I had never seen matched, even in

India. In addition, the people in this Nicaraguan village lived in constant fear that Somoza's regime would kill indiscriminately. An old man approached me and we talked about many things. The beauty of his face spoke eloquently of the dignity of humanity; his eyes reflected the hope that the people's revolution would be successful and peace would come to his village. He talked of his love of life and personal happiness. "But so much suffering," I responded questioningly. "Amor sin dolar no es verdadero amor," he responded in his native Spanish. *Amor sin dolar no es verdadero amor.* The echoes of his words, "love without pain is never true love," have been a constant sermon to me in my life. How well this uneducated but deeply insightful old man knew that adult living is difficult work!

Maturity

As I have indicated in my earlier book, *The Healing Touch of Affirmation,*[1] modern science and theology offer valuable insights into the constituents of maturity. I briefly noted in that book that adult living involves the development of four maturities—physical, intellectual, emotional, and spiritual. I now want to share further insights with regard to emotional and spiritual maturity.

Characteristics of Emotional Maturity

1. Adult living involves growth that provides security and affirmation. As Sigmund Freud pointed out, the emotionally mature person learns not only to love with incompleteness but also to *delay gratification.*

---

1. Thomas A. Kane, *The Healing Touch of Affirmation* (Whitinsville, MA: Affirmation Books, 1976), pp. 52-54.

Not every emotion can be or should be instantly gratified. This also makes adult living painful, because we learn that many times we just cannot have our own way. For the child, gratification must be here and now. The adolescent and adult learn patience and responsible choice and can choose a greater good over personal satisfaction. Understand that I do not mean there is to be *no* gratification; we definitely must have some. We would not eat, or enjoy parties, if we did not know how to gratify ourselves. Obviously, to be psychologically healthy, we need to have more successes than failures. We must enjoy some gratification without guilt, or understand why we cannot have it at this time. But if we listen to the quick-cure talk, we are negating this characteristic of maturity that accepts the fact that gratification will sometimes be delayed.

2. Through interviewing and testing many mature persons and researching their biographies, psychologists have found that these individuals possess a number of similar traits. Emotionally mature persons make *better use of free will* than do those suffering from a lack of affirmation. They are in a better emotional position to make deliberate decisions and choices, because their judgment is not affected by pressing personal needs but focuses rather on the total reality of themselves and the situation. An example of an emotionally immature person is the woman fixated on the need to feel secure who marries a man who may be quite an unsuitable mate, except that he meets her security needs very well. Once married, she either remains stagnated on an infantile level or gets

her security needs filled so well that she no longer "needs" him as security and sees nothing else in him that is particularly attractive. In a sense, she outgrows the basis of the marriage!

3. The third characteristic of the emotionally mature person is an *accurate perception of reality*. Tunnel vision is the possession of the immature; that is, their vision is limited to seeing and hearing things the way they want and sifting out perceptions that threaten their narrow vision. For example, a well-intentioned father may choose to ignore the beginning signs of alcoholism or drug addiction in his son or daughter until it is too late. An emotionally mature person is open to all of reality, the best and the worst. When a person is open to all the possibilities of reality, there are many opportunities for creative responses.

4. *Commitment and fidelity* are characteristics of the emotionally mature person, whether it be to marriage, to priesthood or religious life, or to a principle or a task. Such constancy is impossible for emotionally immature persons, because half of them is always asking, "What's in it for me?" and "What do I lose if it doesn't work out?" The emotionally mature can give themselves totally and do not need to keep one foot outside the door in case of emergencies. The emotional ability to make a commitment is especially important in this day and age, which so often praises "living for the moment." A true commitment is only possible if a person does not totally identify with the present moment.

5. A mature person has a *fresh appreciation for life.*

The immature sink into daily routine and find themselves unchangeable, apathetic, and bored. The world will long remember Angelo Roncalli, Pope John XXIII, and the "fresh air" he brought to Church and society.

I remember my first pastor when I was a newly ordained priest. He was in his seventies, had a zest for life, and was open and notably cheerful. At the same time, I remember a young seminarian of the same parish for whom life was nothing but dullness—he was twenty-four going on ninety-four!

6. Mature people are *transparent*. They allow others to see right through them because they have a minimum of defenses and do not try to cover up thoughts, feelings, motivations, limitations, or weaknesses. They are open, spontaneous, and immediately attracted by a display of personal integrity. However, it is important to emphasize here that by being transparent I do not mean baring our soul to everyone or letting absolutely everyone know us completely. I am not advocating psychological nudity or the "let it all hang out" philosophy. Only a few people will know us completely and this process takes several years. Many of the young people entering ministry today are transparent in a healthy sense. They are open, honest, sincere, and not fearful of acknowledging limitations or human weaknesses.

7. Mature people have a *personal set of convictions;* that is, a unifying philosophy of life. This personal philosophy influences their actions and behavior and helps them to live a life in which principles and convictions are asserted. For example, mature people are

not always trying to please others. They can accept that some people will dislike or reject them because of their religious or humanitarian beliefs.

Because the Church has consistently taught that grace builds on nature, we have begun by briefly considering emotional maturity. Now we know that the person growing emotionally in the life of affirmation is better equipped to take delight in spiritual realities.

Steps to Spiritual Maturity

1. The first step in the journey to spiritual maturity is the awareness that *God intervenes in human history.* For example, he first entered our personal existence by giving us the gift of life. For Christians, he intervenes in baptism, our second birth, and he intervenes in our lives calling us to a particular vocation.

2. The second step on the road to spiritual maturity is the awareness that *God is a faithful God.* He does not take away his love from us. On the other hand, he respects our liberty to accept or refuse his love in all circumstances. He is the Rock whose words and promises will never pass.

3. The third step in the journey toward spiritual maturity is the realization that *God's intervention is a call that demands a response.* Our faith is a remembrance of God's gifts to us and our response to these gifts. None of us can remain insensitive to the love which reaches out to us.

4. The fourth step is the awareness that *God expects an answer* from us. His fidelity calls forth fidelity.

5. The fifth step is the conviction that *faith leads us to*

dedicate ourselves to the service of God. This faith consists of a personal adherence to God, implying an engagement of our whole being. It is the opposite of sin, which is the act of turning away from God. Faith is never compelled by God; it can only be given to him freely. The more we live within the absolute, divine freedom, the freer we are. This experience of faith fulfills some of our most basic needs; it especially helps us to reach out to others by transcending ourselves.[2]

Workaholism

An important sign of maturity in the adult person is perseverance in work. It is certainly true that "hard work has never killed anyone." However, overwork can kill. It can kill physically, emotionally, and spiritually. Overwork can lead to several dangers which impede a life of happiness and affirmation. The schema below points to this process:

functionalism—workaholism $\begin{cases} \text{the burnt-out} \\ \text{the bored} \end{cases}$ alienation

Because as a psychotherapist I work mainly with persons in ministry, I will use them as an example of the point I am attempting to make, although it can certainly be applied to most adults.

Many persons in ministry are so busy *doing* things, working in the name of the Good Shepherd, that they have little time left for *being.* Because they are now fewer in

---

2. Anna Polcino, M.D., "Loneliness: The Genesis of Solitude, Friendship, and Contemplation," *Hospital Progress* (August 1979): 64.

number, those in ministry have taken on more tasks, are attending more meetings, making more pastoral visits, trying to reach out to more people. If I were to make one criticism of priests and religious, bishops and major superiors, I would say they are trying too hard. I am often saddened when I suggest to a group of apostolic ministers that they must take time for leisure if they are going to preserve good spiritual and mental health, and their response is one of smiles, if not laughter, at my simple naivete. Their response conveys to me, "You must have little understanding of the demands placed on those of us in ministry."

Functionalists believe that success in the Lord's work demands complete absorption. They find it difficult, if not impossible, to slow down, to be alone with self, to get away for a day, let alone a vacation. "The work will not survive without me" may become "I cannot survive without the work." Ministry becomes slavery.

Young priests and religious often learn during their first days in ministry that they will win approval from authority figures, from other priests and religious, by being industrious and efficient drudges. The more work they do, the more their superiors will entrust to them. So often when priests and religious gather together they compare notes on what they are doing. The activity in which they engage is more important to them than who they are or who others are. We see many of our colleagues becoming specialists, choosing to work in counseling, ecumenism, social apostolates. They lose themselves in a never-ending litany of projects and causes. This apostolic workaholism is typified by two groups that I often see in my consulting room: the "burnt-out" and the "bored."

The Burnt-Out and The Bored Syndromes

The burnt-out phenomenon is common to many health and social service professionals: lawyers, physicians, social workers, teachers, psychologists, and psychiatrists. These good people, unable or unwilling to set limits on their work, are almost always chronically tired, frustrated, and overextended. They work ceaselessly, but feel a sense of failure. This leads to pain and anger, to hostility and blaming others, to guilt and a wide range of other powerful emotions.

The bored syndrome afflicts those who find that circumstances do not change fast enough in their lives. They are not sufficiently stimulated in their living situation. Boredom is the perceived lack of change in the environment. The amount of change, little or great, actually taking place does not matter; if persons believe there is no change, they are bored. Much apostolic functionalism and workaholism is nothing but a disguised form of boredom.

Working slavishly for the good of souls is often an attempted escape from boredom, never a solution. A person who turns to work or to other activities like sports, travel, parties, or hobbies as an escape from boredom fails to deal with the situation which caused the boredom in the first place. We take ourselves with us wherever we go. Even in prayer we must be careful to discern what is spontaneous from what is merely impulsive.

Functionalism, as typified by the burnt-out and the bored, can lead only to alienation from God and the things of God. This is the lot of many people in ministry today: they are basically unhappy and receive little or no emotional fruit from ministry. They will probably never leave ministry, but will remain in it so tired, so completely drained, that the people they should be ministering to become an interference in their lives, problems to be avoided rather than souls reflecting the presence of God. The functionally oriented life will almost certainly lead to alienation from self, from friends, and from the Church. Little by little, the alienated priests, administrators, and teachers begin to avoid any personal involvement in the duties of their apostolate. They grow less and less open to future growth and become mired in the safe repetition of routine. Eventually, alienated persons begin to sense that others are aware of this deterioration in their attitude. Priests and religious who know they have lost their own sense of dedication begin to resent what they consider the silent reproof in the lives of their sincere colleagues. Jealousy and suspicion make relationships more difficult until ultimately the alienated ministers are out of touch with others as well as themselves.

Invitation to Reflection

In contrast to this depressing picture is the ministry of affirmation, which brings so many opportunities for healing. It is an invitation to life, an approach to living. Although it uses many techniques of psychology and spirituality, affirmation is not a technique but a lifestyle.

Many of us in our work find that we are put in situations where we always have to react. Sometimes we find ourselves bringing this reactive behavior into our personal life. We are unhappy because we are always reacting, not reflecting. Affirmation offers us hope and the possibility of an optimistic solution. It is a conversion experience, an invitation to take the Good Shepherd seriously. Sometimes

I think Christians are so *busy* with their work that they would not recognize the Good Shepherd if he approached them. This busyness stems from an idea prevalent in the Western world, that persons are good only if they are working, producing. Christians are guilty of this fallacy when they define themselves totally in the sense of their work.

Individuals are more than what they do; they are who they are. Unconsciously or not, people sense this. I have had so many people say to me, "I need to be wanted for who I am, not just for what I do." Affirmation speaks to this need, because it is primarily concerned with being and not with doing. If we take the process of affirmation seriously, we will be Christian members of a great counterculture movement, which has been consistently present in our rich Christian tradition, although often clouded in history. In contrast to the functional model of the society in which we live, we will represent a model where persons are accepted and found worthwhile because of who they are.

Because affirmation invites us to emphasize being, there is time for self, for others, and for God. We define the limits of our work so that we have adequate time for prayer, meditation, leisure, and play. Then we move towards an integration in our lives, and work itself becomes more meaningful. We are able to trust the Good Shepherd when he says, "I will not abandon my sheep." We know that if we take care of ourselves with generosity, and if we take care of one another in faith, the Good Shepherd will take care of the Church and our work. He will not abandon us. We will accomplish more than if we labored as if everything depended upon us.

However, as I said earlier, adult living is difficult work. Even though I am affirmed and I affirm others, all of life's problems are not automatically solved. I will experience tension, anxiety, and rebuffs, but because I expect the cross in my life as well as happiness, I will be able to live peacefully. I will be more comfortable because affirmation is an invitation to a life of reflection, and that reflection shows me the value of being as well as doing.

In the next chapter we will see what affirmation means and how this approach to living allows us a reasonable degree of happiness.

Chapter III

"Nice People" Who Deny

You have no idea
What a poor opinion I have
of myself
and
how little I deserve it.

—William S. Gilbert

The opposite of affirmation is denial.

It is easy to recognize and condemn the behavior of the child abuser, the wife beater, or the criminal. Denial is the opposite of affirmation and it is often practiced by the so-called nice people. They have good jobs, material comforts, and many of the "having made it" items of middle- and upper-class America. Yet, these "nice people" many times are too busy to take the time to be present with their children, too busy to communicate effectively with their husbands or wives, too busy to get involved in social justice, just too busy *doing*, striving for position or things that may give them status and apparently never causing open harm to anyone. These "nice people" often excel in the exercise of denial.

A Good Front?

Oh, Americans put up a good front. Listen to child psychiatrist and Pulitzer prize winner Robert Coles: "We have the overwhelming majority of the world's child psychologists and child psychiatrists. Our universities and, increasingly, our high schools devote themselves to a proliferation of courses in child development. . . . Books (and there are dozens of them) like those written by Dr. Spock attract an enormous, eager and sometimes all too gullible readership.

"The prevailing concern of parents is not what the child ought to believe and live up to . . . but what is 'best' for the child. Every effort is made to 'understand' children, even infants under one," Coles wrote in a *Time* magazine bicentennial essay.

On the other hand, Cornell psychologist Urie Bronfenbrenner concluded that "the system for making human beings human in this society is breaking down." Bronfenbrenner, according to an article in *Psychology Today*, "looked at nearly every trend having to do with the well-being of children that you can plot on a graph, and found that factors indicating growth, happiness and effectiveness are on the skids."

Some 1978 statistics from *Current Magazine* support Bronfenbrenner's conclusions. A child born in Hong Kong stands a better chance of living through its first year than one born in Newark, New Jersey, and a white American child stands twice the chance of a black child; more than sixty percent of the sixty million children in the United States receive inadequate medical attention; thirty percent of the country's children are not being inoculated against diseases, and the percentage of children inoculated is even lower in poverty areas; although children represent a third of the country's population, they receive only ten percent of public funds spent on mental health; and two thousand children a year die from physical abuse, often by their own parents.

A 1979 report by the National Commission on Children in Need of Parents stated that half a million children, many of whom do not belong in the foster care system, are presently caught up in the network. Once in the system, they are often shuffled about from home to home, sometimes actually being "lost."

The explanation for the contrast between what Americans claim to want for their children and what they, collectively, give them, said Margaret Mead, may lie in the discontinuity between generations. When pioneering immigrants came to America, they looked to their children as the promise of the future. Parents worked and sacrificed so that their children's lives would be better than their own. Not every child could succeed, however. Many parents, at a loss for faith themselves, had none to pass on to their progeny.

"Large sections of the population ceased to believe in the possibility of mobility and reared their children with low expectations and little hope," Mead wrote. By the 1950s, the expectation that children would fulfill their parents' dreams was being shared by a smaller and smaller percentage of the population. "A larger proportion was settling into a life of fatalistic desperation in which the price of crops, the vagaries of employment, the business cycle, the half-dug subways, the inflammable buildings, the weather, the corruption in high places and the ethical inconsistencies of undeclared wars all blended together as a kind of inescapable fate.''

According to Mead, the optimism drought, coupled with the new emphasis on nonparenthood generated by the Zero Population Growth movement in the 1960s, may have been enough to do in children. ''We have become,'' she continued, ''a society of people who neglect our children, are afraid of our children, find children surplus instead of the raison d'être.'' Even the children of the vast American middle class, who grew up with swing sets in the backyard and bicycles in the carport, with their own bedrooms and bathrooms and, at sixteen, their own cars, have paid a price for their material gains.

Denial of Children

''We have continued to misuse children as instruments of pride and power, instead of recognizing them as human beings with needs of their own.'' Because children can no longer pay with labor in the family fields, they are expected to make themselves worthwhile in parental pleasure. ''Children,'' Mead stated, ''have become instruments of adult aggrandizement.''

The very adults who expect to gain so much joy and satisfaction from their own children often fail to see or attempt to meet the needs of other children, the little bodies and minds behind the statistics on poverty and abuse. If even parents are often blind to the deficiencies in children's lives, the sixty percent of the country's adults who have no

children living at home are even less perceptive and
sympathetic.

More and more often, public policy, influenced greatly
by this majority, is to cut taxes and expenses where they
would hurt children the most, in school and welfare programs. "We are a representational democracy in which our
leaders determine the use of resources and the laws by
which we live in accordance with the wishes of their constituents, the voters," said Leslie Dashew Isaacs, director
of consultation and education for the Central Fulton Community Mental Health Center in Atlanta, Georgia. "Children are the largest under-represented minority in the
country. Without the clout of votes and financial contributions, children's rights and needs are often neglected. By
law, children are still seen as the 'property' of their
parents, with only recent gains regarding protection
against violence of parents. Nor have national resources
been allocated with children in mind. Inflation-conscious
congressmen are likely to cut funds for children before
higher priority funds are touched. Thus, if we look realistically at the manner in which we are represented by our
leaders, children are not our main concern."

"The truth is that every child on the planet is the responsibility of every adult," Alison Kilgour of *Newsweek*
wrote in an essay, "What's Wrong With Kids?" "The inability or unwillingness to recognize this and act on it, even
on a very small scale, is, and there is no other word for it,
childish. If maturity can be defined by the amount of responsibility we're willing to take on and be able to handle,
then it would seem that the problem here is not kids; the
problem is big, overgrown kids in adults' clothing who for

unattractively selfish reasons are trying to weasel out of one of life's main duties: looking out for the real children."

Nobel prize winner Gabriela Mistra expressed the sentiment more poetically:

> We are guilty of many errors and many faults, but
> Our worst crime is abandoning the children,
> Neglecting the fountain of life.
> Many of the things we need can wait.
> The child cannot.
> Now is the time his bones are formed;
> His blood is constituted;
> His senses are being developed.
> We cannot answer him "Tomorrow."
> His name is "Today."

Openness to New Life

The purpose of discussing at length our attitudes toward children is to point to the need to affirm rather than deny. Persons or even nations who are not open to new life will ultimately find themselves wondering why they have lives in which nobody says, "I love you."

People are more important than things. If society is going to emphasize only material benefits and not give witness to justice, generosity, and selflessness, then it surely is on a road to self-destruction.

The Denied Speak

Listen to the biographical statements that some of my clients have written over the years. In order to preserve the anonymity of these clients, these are composite reflections.

> I was the youngest of five children and my father never really accepted me. He called me "the mistake" and

really didn't even like me to be at the same table for meals. When the rest of the family went on vacation, I stayed with my aunt and uncle. Like my mother, they made me feel important, but I always felt ugly or dirty because of my father's reaction to me. I wanted to play baseball with my dad as he had done with my other brothers, but I would never dare ask him. Eventually, things got so bad my parents broke up. I still think of myself as "the mistake" who ruined our family life.

—Male University Student

My mother and father argued almost daily. It was always about money. Even though he was a physician and made a good salary at a specialized hospital, he would give my mother little money. He treated mother as if she were a schoolgirl. She was so frightened of him, she'd never speak up. He used to boast how thrifty she was and how trustful. Dad would go away on business trips, always for seemingly noble purposes, and never told us where he was going. He'd call home periodically to see if everything was all right. Dad would really not be concerned with some of his patients that came to the house-office. But, if they paid well, they'd get excellent treatment. He thought he was teaching us something about money by being so miserly. He said in the "old country" he had to go without so much. He had little time to be with us. We wouldn't answer back for fear of his wrath. Yet, he never hurt us or abused us. I just know that as a teenager I grew to hate men because of the image of a man my father gave me.

—Female High School Student

When I was eight years old, I was sent to boarding school. During vacations, I always told my parents how wonderful it was and how much I loved it. Really, I hated it and in my heart pleaded they wouldn't send me back. The other girls at the school seemed happy and the teachers were kind, but somehow I just could never understand why my parents would send their only daughter five hundred miles away when there were excellent schools in our own city. They gave me attention while I was with them, but each time I left to go off to school again I felt they were breathing a sigh of relief.

—Female School Teacher

As long as I can remember, I have felt rejected by my parents. I always felt they never wanted me and that the best thing I could do would be not to bother them. I remember more than once they told me that they didn't think I was their child and that there must have been a mix-up at the hospital. Someone else got their baby and they ended up with me. When I told them at fourteen that I wanted to enter the convent, they suddenly changed their attitudes and became proud of me. But when I left the convent at eighteen years of age, they said they never wanted to see me again. They almost destroyed me.

—Female Office Worker

A few weeks after I was ordained a priest, I was assigned to a parish in a lovely country town. The people welcomed me, but from the first day I stepped into the rectory, I could tell I was not welcomed by the pastor. He'd pass comments about my appearance, about my mixing with the laity, about my taking time off to play tennis, and so on. I just couldn't seem to do anything right. I tried to talk with him, but was put down by "in my house you'll do things my way." His way was to be the center of attention, his recreation was gossip or the television. His constant concern was that the phone "be guarded" because someone might call and need a priest. We got two emergency calls in a whole year. He was a good preacher and most of the people liked him. However, he was a lonely man and disguised his lack of friends by excessive work. I didn't have to ask for a transfer; he went to the bishop without even telling me.

Unfortunately, I heard about my transfer by way of rumors long before the bishop called me to his office. Thank God for an understanding bishop, and now my new assignment is a good one. But still, I feel very angry that my first assignment was full of put-downs.

—*Young Priest*

Sister Provincial assigned me to teach the eighth grade in a large urban parish. It was a good assignment and I enjoyed it. But before long, I was asked to do so many different jobs in the school, the parish, and for our religious congregation that I got very depressed. I just cannot say no. Yet, this work is killing me. No one seems to care. I'm needed because I do my work well, but I constantly feel I'm really unwanted as an individual. I'm tired of being a functionary. I need some time for leisure and prayer, but when I do take a little time, I feel guilty. I just feel as if I'm falling apart and I don't want my emotional life to hurt the children I teach. I want to be a good nun. I want to serve the Church. I want to work hard. I want friends. I don't want to run away from my cross in life, but feel others are pressing me and I'm allowing myself to be pushed to the breaking point.

—*Religious Teacher*

I can't believe I killed my baby. Yes, I had an abortion just so I wouldn't shame our fine Catholic family. I wasn't married and the man involved had no intention of marrying me. We really don't love each other. I feel that I am no good and that life promises me nothing but unhappiness, because of what I did. I went to the birth control clinic frightened. Only the baby's father knew I was going to the clinic. The counselor at the clinic told me that what I was doing was the right thing and that at nineteen I had my own life to consider. Never did the counselor help me to consider the alternatives. I felt so alone and made a quick decision. I'm angry that I never told my family because, looking back, I'm sure they would have helped me confront reality and they would have supported me. I am angry at the baby's father for what he called the result of "recreational sex." I am angry at the counselor at the clinic. I am so angry at myself and at how terrible a person I must be to do what I have done.

—Female Factory Worker

I came from a home that was warm and loving. Shortly after I married my husband, I noticed he saw little need for me to remain an "individual." More and more, he considered me to be part of himself, taking me for granted. He just presumed his wishes were my wishes. He never discussed plans with me or ever even considered that I might have an independent thought or feeling. Often he told me, by action and word, that I was there to serve him. He just used me. He treated me like a thing, like something he owned. Even after he died in an automobile accident, I found myself thinking, "What would Charlie expect of me now?"

—Married Woman, Mother

I came from a happy home. Mom and dad were fully present to us. All four kids and our parents enjoyed doing things together and being together. When I was about six, I can remember being attracted to other boys and men. I never told anyone and my adolescence was marked by severe guilt and fear that people would find out that I was different. I starred on the high school basketball team and, to keep up appearances, I dated girls frequently. It wasn't until college that I acknowledged my homosexuality and decided that I was in love with another man. I was not permissive and tried to be responsible. I decided to tell my parents, who were still my number one fans. When I did, dad kicked me out of the house and said he would never speak to his queer son again. Mom was hostile for the first time in my life. I couldn't believe my parents would do such a thing. Deep down I wondered if they ever did love me or just the good things I had done to bring attention to them. Five years later and my good parents won't allow me into their home until I leave my lover. I only wish my parents would allow me to be myself and respect my adult choices.

—Male Law Student

My wife, after two years of marriage, began to be very critical of me and my work. Because of the political structure of my work situation, it was apparent I would not be able to climb the executive ladder. But, I was getting a good salary and enjoyed my position—advancement meant more money and prestige, but that was all as far as I was concerned, and it wasn't worth it. My wife became abusive in the manner in which she related to me. When she found out I could not father children, she became even more negative. At parties or visiting relatives, she would openly insult me or pass cutting comments. Oftentimes she'd go for days without having any kind of conversation with me. Yes, she got the meals, kept a nice house, and was pleasing in that way. Things got worse. I tried and friends suggested to her that she get counseling. She wouldn't hear of it. Eventually we separated, but I am still left with the haunting feeling of having disappointed the person I loved most in life.

—Male Business Administrator

My professor became very impressed with me and my research. Though married and having a family, he was a lonely man, even though he was a sought-after lecturer and popular in certain circles. He guided my research and we became good friends. I began to notice that his motives were less than sincere and that basically he wanted to control my life. He needed admirers and not a research assistant. When I started to withdraw from his personal attention, he threatened to ruin me professionally. He said I was plagiarizing his research. He even got the university to bring the matter to civil court. He became very paranoid and would do what he could to hurt me in his writings and lectures. Fortunately, people began to notice his illness and didn't take him seriously. Unfortunately, he would never seek treatment and continues to manipulate people. I grieve that he is such a lonely person. I must look into myself to see why I allowed myself to be so victimized.

—*Male College Instructor*

What is Denial?

There are many ways to explain the personal experience of denial. Persons who feel denied have the awareness that someone does not love them, does not want them, is not interested in them.

Most denied persons felt as children that they had no personal worth. A child who has this experience of denial will constantly struggle in life against a sense of not being wanted or of being inadequate and insecure. The adult who was denied affirmation as a child is characterized by an inability to establish satisfying emotional rapport with other adults, resulting in a lack of genuine friendship, excessive loneliness, and failure in marriage and personal life.

Many denied persons do achieve in occupational and professonal life. They are good "doers." Feeling inferior to others, they try to compensate by showing others and themselves that they are important. They do this through acquiring material possessions; seeking fame; controlling others (through money, politics, and so forth); or compulsive sexual experimenting.

Affirmation allows the opportunity for a person to grow emotionally. However, it is denial, not affirmation, when one backslaps and gives undeserved praise and sugary and superficial compliments. Such shallow attempts seemingly to affirm are recognized as denial and only add to self-doubt, guilt, depression, and interpersonal ineffectiveness.

In the next chapter, we will reflect on the psychotheology of affirmation and how it offers insight and the possibility of healing.

Affirmation—A Journey Toward Happiness

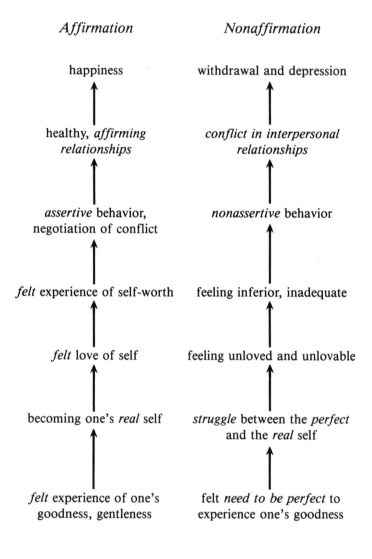

Affirmation	*Nonaffirmation*
happiness	withdrawal and depression
↑	↑
healthy, *affirming* relationships	*conflict in interpersonal relationships*
↑	↑
assertive behavior, negotiation of conflict	*nonassertive* behavior
↑	↑
felt experience of self-worth	feeling inferior, inadequate
↑	↑
felt love of self	feeling unloved and unlovable
↑	↑
becoming one's *real* self	*struggle* between the *perfect* and the *real* self
↑	↑
felt experience of one's goodness, gentleness	felt *need to be perfect* to experience one's goodness

If we are ever to be happy in life,
now is the time.
Today should always be our
most wonderful day.

　　　　　　　　—Thomas A. Kane

Chapter IV

The Psychotheology of Affirmation

The primordial affirmation of the Christian anthropology is that man is God's image and cannot be reduced to a mere portion of nature or a nameless element in the human city.

—Pope John Paul II

An important scriptural illustration of the meaning of affirmation is found in the account of the meeting of Jesus and Zacchaeus, the tax collector. Zacchaeus had never been accepted or loved simply for being himself, and evidently he placed some hope in Jesus of Nazareth. Trying to get a view of Jesus as he passed through the neighborhood, Zacchaeus—small in stature—could not work his way through the crowd. He climbed a fig tree at the side of the road hoping to view the Nazarene. Jesus did not pass him by but accepted him as he was. "Zacchaeus, come down because I must stay with you today," Jesus called out to

51

the little man in the tree. What was the result? Zacchaeus immediately opened—like a flower in bloom. He stood there, and said to the Lord: "Here and now, I give away half of my possessions to charity, and if I have cheated anyone, I am ready to repay him four times over" (Luke 19:1-8). Charity and justice, then, are the fruits of the person who has been affirmed and liberated; so too with the person who has been redeemed by Jesus Christ.

To Make Strong

The word affirmation comes from the Latin *affirmare*, and means to make firm, to give strength, to make strong. Affirmation implies assent, agreement, consent, a willingness to say yes to all creation.

Affirmation is the acceptance of the goodness of the other as that person is. Affirmation is at the center of all maturing love. "You are good." "You are wonderful." The healing touch of affirmation means I encourage persons to be who they are, immaturity and shortcomings included, so that their potential may be realized. In reality, when affirmed I receive the gift of myself from another person.

Being, not Doing

Affirmation is concerned primarily with being, not doing. The psychotheology of affirmation goes beyond the workaholism and functionalism so often found in our world. Basically, affirmation produces happiness as found in the Genesis theme, "God saw all he had made, and indeed it was very good" (Gen. 1:31). Note that affirmation reflects the goodness of a person back to that individual. You are good because you are you; because you have great worth in being your unique self. Good, not primarily because you have done anything, or accomplished a great deal, or proven you are successful; no, just because you are you. You are "the apple of God's eye"!

Cocreator

Affirmation is the cocreation we are all called upon to share with God.[1] We are in a real sense creators of one another and of our universe. It is almost as if God creates the human person and leaves it to other humans to bring that person to the fullness of the individual's potentialities. The initial act of creation is always incomplete, and it cannot be finished until we affirm one another into the completeness of the work God has begun.

Approach to Living

Recently I received a letter from Australia from someone requesting literature about the techniques of affirmation and how they are applied to counseling. Of course, I had to respond, as I do to many similar requests, that I do not believe affirmation is a technique nor is there a series of techniques leading to affirmation that I could teach. Affirmation is an approach to life; it is a way of living, a lifestyle. Affirmation is the source of light on our journey toward emotional and spiritual maturity.

Affirmation is Relationship

Earlier, I pointed out that the one necessary ingredient for happiness is some kind of intimate relationship. It is,

---

1. Josef Pieper, *About Love*, (Chicago, IL: Franciscan Herald Press, 1974), p. 25.

then, in terms of relationship that we reflect upon the process of affirmation.

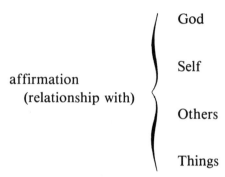

affirmation
(relationship with)

God

Self

Others

Things

Affirmation is Relationship with Things

One of the important aspects of Christian teaching is that things are good as they were created by God for our respectful use. As we begin to grow in affirmation, we notice the development within us of a deep sense of reverence and appreciation for all of creation. We begin with the beauty of the world around us, the majesty of the ocean, the wonder of even one drop of water. Remember, affirmation means to make firm, to make strong. In our relationship with the things of the world, we grow firm, sensitive to the dignity of creation and the awesomeness of the Creator.

Saint Francis of Assisi

Saint Francis of Assisi is an outstanding example of a man who was caught up in the goodness of things, in the beauty around him. Through Francis, we are taught to see the goodness of God in all of creation. His penetrating sense of God's presence produced incredible responses on every level of animate and inanimate nature. It seems as if God restored to this little, poor man, Francis, the affirmation over nature that Adam had surrendered in paradise. This affirmation of creation is beautifully expressed in Francis of Assisi's "Canticle of Brother Sun":

Most High, omnipotent, good Lord,
To you alone belong praise and glory,
Honor and blessing.
No man is worthy to breathe your name.

Be praised, my Lord, for all your creatures.

In the first place for the blessed Brother Sun,
Who gives us the day and enlightens us through you.
He is beautiful and radiant with his great splendor,
Giving witness of you, Most Omnipotent One.

Be praised, my Lord, for Sister Moon and the stars
Formed by you so bright, precious and beautiful.

Be praised, my Lord, for Brother Wind
And the airy skies, so cloudy and serene;
For every weather, be praised, for it is life-giving.

Be praised, my Lord, for Sister Water,
So necessary yet so humble, precious and chaste.

Be praised, my Lord, for Brother Fire,
Who lights up the night.
He is beautiful and carefree, robust and fierce.

Be praised, my Lord, for our sister, Mother Earth,
Who nourishes us and watches us
While bringing forth abundance of fruits
With colored flowers and herbs.

*Be praised, my Lord, for those who pardon through
   your love
And bear weakness and trial.
Blessed are those who endure in peace,
For they will be crowned by you, Most High.*

*Be praised, my Lord, for our sister, Bodily Death,
Whom no living man can escape.
Woe to those who die in sin.
Blessed are those who discover your holy will.
The second death will do them no harm.*

*Praise and bless my Lord.
Render thanks.
Serve him with great humility.*

Amen[2]

Affirmation makes us look at trees and brooks and the desert in a new way. I have my consulting office about thirty miles outside the city of Boston. As my clients progress in the process of affirmation, as their emotional life matures, I always notice less of an emphasis on gathering, hoarding, or just using objects. They develop a respectful presence to things and nature. Frequently, my clients remark: "Today, suddenly for the first time in my life, as I was driving here from Boston, I noticed what a beautiful countryside we have here in New England. I didn't have to listen to news on the radio or to the latest cassette tape, as I was driving. I just looked at scenery, at the picturesque wooden houses, the white frame churches, the rolling stone walls." Such is an affirming posture, that is, acknowledging and enjoying the goodness of creation.

---

2. Brennan Manning, *The Wisdom of Accepted Tenderness* (Danville, NJ: Dimension Books, 1978), pp. 22-23.

I also notice in the process of therapy in our centers that men and women, once they start feeling better about themselves, become more careful about physical appearance, the clothes they select, the way they groom themselves, and the manner in which they decorate their rooms. There is a certain emphasis in our therapeutic communities on atmosphere, because the things with which we surround ourselves show how we feel about ourselves, and speak to the way in which we will affirm others.

Alcohol and Tobacco

Since growth and maturity are often portrayed in our affirmation relationship with nature and things, we might get lost in a dream of simply contemplating the beauty of nature. There is also the hard reality to be faced. We cannot grow in affirmation if we abuse things. Alcohol and tobacco are probably the two most frequently abused items in the world today. Persons cannot mature in affirmation if they abuse alcohol, tobacco, or even food.

Ecology and Environment

In the 1960s, the so-called flower children were often laughed at by many people. They were pointing to the need to respect water, air, and in general, our natural resources. In many ways, they were insisting upon a fundamental Judeo-Christian value of affirming the goodness of the things God gave us to use. Only very gradually are we returning to this respect for nature. As a result of the disrespect and misuse of our planet's resources, we find the following news story in one of today's newspapers:

Washington—Mass poverty, malnutrition, overcrowding, food shortages and deterioration of the planet's water and atmosphere resources—that's a bleak government prediction that says civilization has perhaps twenty years to act to head off such a worldwide disaster.

The three-year U.S. government study released today warned that the world faced those grim problems unless nations cooperated as never before to head them off.

In response to the "Global 2000 Report to the President," President Carter has written top government officials that "unless nations of the world take prompt, decisive action to halt the current trends, the next twenty years may see a continuation of serious food and population problems, steady loss of croplands, forests, plant and animal species, fisheries, and degradation of the earth's water and atmosphere."

The presidential report estimated real food prices would double and energy prices more than double by the turn of the century.

Increasing Stress

The report said its findings "point to increasing potential for international conflict and increasing stress on international financial arrangements." Despite some economic growth, it said, the gap between rich and poor will grow wider.

And the study, headed by the President's Council on Environmental Quality and the State Department, said that, if anything, it was probably too optimistic. President Carter, who ordered the study in 1977, immediately announced appointment of a

Presidential Task Force on Global Resources and Environment to recommend new, top-priority studies "as soon as possible" and to provide a progress report within six months.

The report did not suggest specific policies, but concluded that "substantial economic development, coupled with environmental protection, resources management and family planning, is essential."

Among Findings

The report included these findings:

—World food production may increase ninety percent from 1970 to the year 2000, but population will swell more than fifty-nine percent from some four billion in 1975 to about 6.35 billion in 2000.

—Per capita food production, therefore, will increase only about fifteen percent and those already eating well will get most of the increase, leaving the poor of South Asia, the Middle East and Africa with little more food, and maybe less, than they get now.

—Farmland will increase only about four percent; increased food production must rely on techniques using oil and natural gas, causing food prices to spiral upward along with energy prices.

—"There will be fewer resources to go around," the report says, adding, "Resource-based inflationary pressures will continue and intensify."

—"Regional water shortages will become more severe" because of forest destruction and increased demand.

–*"Extinctions of plant and animal species will increase dramatically. Hundreds of thousands of species—perhaps as many as twenty percent of all species on earth—will be irretrievably lost as their habitats vanish, especially in tropical forests."*[3]

Affirmation is Relationship with Others

Affirmation is basically the complete acceptance of others as they are with both their positive and negative qualities. However, affirmatioin is not mere acceptance; it means that we also choose to help others to develop their potential. In other words, we are always aware that the other person has possibilities not yet developed.

Affirmation is never possession. Of course, as we grow in intimacy with another person, the very natural tendency is to want to control the person, not necessarily in a selfish way, but because we are so sure of who that person should be growing to be. In every relationship we have to wrestle with the problem of possession. Husbands and wives do this all the time. It is particularly difficult for them when one partner grows in a direction that the other does not understand, or fears. The dependent young girl matures into a confident young woman who has a mind of her own and does not always bend to her husband's expectations. What seemed a minor fault of character in the young man becomes more pronounced and threatens to overshadow their relationship. Despite the difficulties, both must struggle against the tendency to possess the other.

---

3. *The Evening Gazette,* Worcester, MA, July 24, 1980, p. 1.

Personality

Human personality, as such, does not exist nor does it grow or develop in a vacuum. Other personalities are needed. Some contend that a sound does not exist unless it is perceived. The fall of a large tree in a forest is translated into sound only when the stimuli of the impact produce an effect on the auditory apparatus of a person or animal.

In the same way, affirmation in the social sense does not exist unless the individual is involved in social relationships with others. This implies constant communications among individuals. These communications or messages originate in one human being, are sent out, reach their destination, and are interpreted and find their expression, realization, or consummation in other human beings. Normal human life cannot exist without human interactions. Let me illustrate this point.

Frederick, an emperor of the Holy Roman Empire during the thirteenth century, wondered what language Adam and Eve spoke in the Garden of Eden. Was it Greek, Hebrew, or Latin? He reasoned that they must have created their own language and form of communication out of necessity.

Frederick thought he might be able to recreate the circumstances under which Adam and Eve had learned to speak. He took a small group of infants and from the moment of their birth isolated them from the speech of others. He instructed wet nurses to remain absolutely silent throughout all of their contacts with the infants. The children, therefore, would never hear human speech until they produced their own.

The emperor never acquired the information he was seeking because all of the children died. The cause of their death remains unknown. It is conceivable that some type of infectious disease or physical illness intervened. One cannot help but wonder whether these children failed to survive primarily because they lacked physical resistance to disease or because they lacked warm, meaningful human contact.

There is support for the latter interpretation in modern counterparts of this situation which demonstrate the necessity of human interpersonal contact for survival.[4] During the mid 1940s, Rene A. Spitz studied ninety-one infants in a foundling home. They were provided with certain material needs such as good food, clothing, light, air, toys, and competent nursing care. Each nurse had eight children and as the report pointed out, each infant had the equivalent of one-eighth of a mother. This was not enough.

Spitz found that thirty percent of the infants died of various causes in their first year, and many of those who survived developed a series of physical, intellectual, and emotional disorders. These disorders were directly related to their age at the time of leaving the foundling home; that is, the longer they were in the home, and the longer they had been treated so impersonally, the greater was the degree of personality impoverishment or susceptibility to physical illness.

Loveless Vacuum

In 1956, John Lilly, a neurophysiologist at the National Institutes of Health in Washington, D.C., demonstrated dramatically that sudden and complete isolation of a

---

4. Jack Dominian, M.D., *Cycles of Affirmation* (London: Darton, Longman and Todd, Ltd., 1975).

mature, emotionally stable individual from all meaningful external stimuli creates sufficient degrees of overwhelming stress to cause temporary pathological reactions. Human volunteers, isolated under experimental conditions from people and things, lost contact with their environment and with themselves. They developed strange and unreal sensations, hallucinated, became fearful, and lost their ability to concentrate, to remember, and to exercise good judgment. When they withdrew from the experiment and resumed normal contact with their environment, their previous personalities returned—another graphic illustration of the extent to which we are dependent upon others for survival and for our normal functioning.

Senior Citizens

We also recognize how important it is for older persons to be in touch with familiar people and things. An aged person who, for either physical or social reasons, is deprived of meaningful human contact fades away. Some older folks lose their sense of reality and, ultimately, their sense of themselves. For example, when older persons are removed from their normal home situation and are placed in strange surroundings, such as a nursing home, hospital, or the home of a younger member of the family, difficulties can ensue. Frequently older persons become quite disoriented at night, cannot find their way around, and consequently may become very confused.

Thus, it is sound nursing procedure, whether the aged persons are in a nursing home, hospital, or another new location, to leave a light burning at night in their room so that they can orient themselves to the new situation. The light keeps familiar objects ever in view. Darkness, on the other hand, makes these objects disappear, and feelings of fear and confusion are likely to occur.

Communication

We do need others in order to live. Human society and human personality cannot exist without human relationships. We need other people at every level and degree of relationship, one-to-one, one-to-two, and one-to-many—in our personal lives, in our families, and in our community. Modern life necessitates the development of many complex relationships and upon the structure of these relationships lies the meaning of life. To express it differently, we need to be affirmed by others and we need to affirm others if life is to have any meaning or significance.

However, before we can achieve any relationship to others, we must be able to communicate with them. In meaningful human relationships, the individuals are of emotional importance to each other; they are ready to understand and to respond to each other's needs.

Our well-being depends upon our being continuously in touch with those about us. We learn about ourselves by seeing the reactions of others to us and by observing the feelings we arouse in them. We establish our identity by bringing ourselves into harmony with others. This is achieved through the process of affirmation.

Psychotherapy

In recent years, psychotherapists have been interested in this process of interpersonal communication, for it is generally recognized that communication is a primary tool of therapy and that in the establishment of the therapeutic relationship, the importance of communication cannot be overestimated. Many nonaffirmed clients have particular difficulties in communicating; they feel cut off from any kind of relatedness to others.

This is part of their reaction to life's circumstances and, in fact, part of their illness. They feel that they are not understood by their family and by others in their own community. Not only are their communications with others at times seriously impaired, but also their own understanding of themselves. We can recognize this, in a way, by observing the difficulties which individuals often have in accepting some of their own ideas and accomplishments or lack thereof, and their inability to explain satisfactorily to themselves some of their own actions.

The aim of psychotherapy, therefore, is to help clients communicate with others in a more satisfactory way and to help them to be able to examine various aspects of their own mental functioning. Consequently, members of the various professions whose work is concerned with people as human beings must have particular sensitivity, skill, and respect for the process of communication between people.

Materialism

Perhaps one reason why modern persons feel lonely and helpless at times is that they have tended, especially in some societies, to lose themselves in the world of material comfort. They have lost sight of their own human qualities and of themselves as persons with unique feelings, capacities, and relationships. For individuals to fulfill their potential and to function optimally, they must communicate at all levels: the physical, the psychological, the personal, the social, and the spiritual.

Persons who suffer from a lack of affirmation have special problems communicating with others. Often the problems stem from faulty communication between the parents and the child. Such disturbances in childhood may spring from severe anxiety, especially when the child is unable to understand the desires of the parents. There may be a secondary effect, in that the inability to understand may intensify the anxiety, laying the basis within the personality for the future formation of symptoms of emotional illness.

Alienation

Many persons who suffer from a lack of affirmation have in common that, above all else, they experience feelings of loneliness, separation, and isolation. These alienated people have some type of deprivation of affection or difficulty in interpersonal relationships. The experience of isolation gives rise to the most painful emotion which human beings may have to endure—*alienation*.

Because the human mind tends to avoid repetition of painful feelings and experiences, it sets mechanisms into operation which will protect the individual against future recurrences of hurt, injury, or rejection. This may result in several attitudes or types of behavior.

One of these is a "touch me not" reaction, a pattern of withdrawal from social contacts. It is almost as if the individual reasons, "If people have been unkind and unaccepting of me, and have hurt me in such a way, I will have nothing to do with them." "If I do not go near the fire, I will not get burnt."

Another way a person may react is with an attitude of pseudo-independence. Such behavior is nothing more than a denial of the painful experience of isolation. It is a reaction of "I don't need anybody. I am a free and independent agent. By doing things myself, I will not get hurt by others."

Some persons may handle this problem of aloneness in yet another manner by behaving towards others as they wish they would be treated. This can lead to a type of pseudo-altruism. These persons operate on the basis of "If I continuously give to others or try to please others, maybe they will like me."

Some people have an intense fear of loneliness and isolation even when superficially there is no apparent cause for such concern. At a deeper level, however, to be without aims in life, to be without goals for which to work, and to be without others with whom to work for common ends are some of the basic causes for feelings of isolation.

In addition to the fear of aloneness or separation, other emotions which interfere with acceptance of others are anxiety and anger. Harry Stack Sullivan defined anxiety as fear of anticipated loss of love or approval through separation, social isolation, or disruption of personal relationships upon which one is dependent. The feeling of anxiety may also accompany feelings of alienation. Common to both is a lack of affirmation in human relationships.[5]

Acceptance of others through affirmation is an ideal of our Church and society. Perhaps all that has been said can be expressed best by the old Hindu proverb, "Help thy brother's boat across, and lo! thine own has reached the shore."

---

5. Harold I. Kaplan, Alfred M. Freedman, Benjamin J. Sadock, *Comprehensive Textbook of Psychiatry,* 3rd ed., vol. 2, (London: Williams and Wilkins, 1980), pp. 1,310-12.

The Significant Other

In order to achieve full maturity, persons must develop close relationships and yet retain their own individuality. To grow emotionally mature a person must receive acceptance by others. In the mutuality of being affirmed and affirming others, individuals enhance their ability to give of themselves to others. Without affirmation of others, there cannot be affirmation by others.

The *significant other* is that beautiful human person who reflects my goodness back to me. My significant other, though aware of my shortcomings and immaturity, compels me to take joy in being myself and challenges my potential for growth. I know that this person loves me and is not concerned with using me. We grow in appreciation of self through the affirmation of significant others.

I would like to present once again the following outline on significant others which first appeared in *The Healing Touch of Affirmation:*[6]

Developmental Stage	Significant Others
In the womb	Mother
Infancy	Mother primarily, and father
Preschool years	Parents, older brothers and sisters, relatives
Early school years.	Same as above, but now enter other significant adults, such as teachers, clergy, etc.

---

6. Kane, *The Healing Touch of Affirmation*, p. 42.

Adolescent years ... Family closeness important; friends now
affirm
The Parental Proclamation:
"You are you."
"You are a worthwhile individual."

College years ...... Friends, other loves now affirm
significantly.

Marriage.......... Two mature adults affirm one another.

Celibate style ...... Definite need to develop close emotional
bonds with women and men friends.

Middle years....... Husband, wife, friends, and children
reflect back to parents their own
goodness.

Retirement years ... Husband, wife, children, and other
caring persons

Masculine and Feminine

Most of the world's adults will be affirmed by a member
of the opposite sex. A small part of the world's population
will be affirmed by a member of the same sex; and, by this
statement I do not mean only persons with a homosexual
orientation.

One of the most important contributions to the contemporary understanding of ourselves as men and women has
come from Carl Jung, the Swiss psychiatrist. Jung's writings have helped us to understand not only the differences
in the psychology of men and women but also how the
sexes interrelate and how the male and female in each of us
affects our relationships.

The following quote is taken from a letter by the bishops
of this country entitled "As One Who Serves." Though
written to American priests, I believe it can teach all of us.

Too often, stress which has been placed on avoiding relationships effects a defensive style when priests relate with women, or when sisters relate with men, either socially or in ministry. Such style is particularly inappropriate today when men and women are expected to interact on a regular basis as co-workers as well as in social situations.

Men and women must be able to interact in relationships which are mature, honest, responsible and appreciative. Such relationships presume a realistic degree of self-knowledge. Furthermore, they allow each person to realize his or her God-given dignity in the blend of femininity and masculinity within every person. This blend is God's gift to us and to each other. Men and women who are church ministers, as much as any other human persons, need one another's support in personal development. Celibate commitment must be a path toward the sort of independence, self-reliance and wholeness which make one capable of conscious self-sacrificing and loving relationships with others. Otherwise, it cannot be an appropriate lifestyle.[7]

Affirmation of your Neighbor

While we are stating that affirmation is relationship with others, we would be remiss if we did not remind ourselves that as Christians we are called upon to see love of neighbor as primary in our religion.

Jesus stated this unequivocally: "I give you a new commandment: love one another. Such as my love has been for you, so must your love be for each other. This is how all will know you for my disciples: your love for one another" (John 13:34-35).

---

7. U.S. Bishops, Committee on Priestly Life and Ministry, *As One Who Serves* (Washington, DC: U.S.C.C., 1977), p. 65.

What characterized Jesus' love for people? His was a completely unselfish and indiscriminate love, a love which was expressed by the giving of his very self "to the end" (John 13:1).

For this reason the cross is the universal symbol of the Christian, not because it was an instrument of torture, but because it sums up the life, the whole earthly existence of Jesus—a life marked from beginning to end by love of his Father and very active love of his brothers and sisters. This is the cross which he told Christians they must carry if they really wanted to be his disciples.

When Jesus was challenged to commit himself on the question of the greatest commandment of the law, he unhesitatingly replied with the command to love God as stated in Deuteronomy 6:5. He was quick to add, however, "The second is like it: 'You shall love your neighbor as yourself.' " He went on, very pointedly, to insist, "On these two commandments the whole law is based, and the prophets as well" (Matt. 22:37-40).

In Luke's versions of this dialogue, Jesus' questioner pressed him for further precision: "And who is my neighbor?" (10:29). Jesus' very familiar answer was not a dictionary definition of neighbor, but the parable of the Good Samaritan. Its point would have been shockingly clear to his audience. It said, in effect, that the concept of neighbor could not really be defined, because it was not limited by considerations of blood relationship or ethnic ties or by arbitrary restrictions of any kind.

Every human person is a neighbor for whom our love is encouraged as second in importance only to love of God. As Jesus says in Mark's version (12:31), "There is no other commandment greater than these "

Jesus told us that we are to be the salt of the earth and the light of the world. But if this light never shines beyond the walls of our houses or the fences of our backyards, then we are hiding it "under a bushel basket" (Matt. 5:15), the very thing Jesus warned us not to do. For if Christians hide their light, what hope is there of transforming society?

It is not difficult to see the connection between psychological truths and the gospel of Jesus Christ. Central to his teaching is the notion of entering into relationship with other people and of loving them. The enormous energy generated by his teaching (which was crowned by his life and death "for his brethren") was an energy of affirmation. The apostles went out to love the world and teach all persons that they could and must make the effort to love humanity. We know that the initial mission was successful by the fact that we teach and try to practice the Christian message today.

Affirmation is Relationship with Self

When I say affirmation is relationship with self, I mean that persons possess a known and felt awareness of their own inner goodness. Affirmation is a respectful love of self. We are lovable not because of our self-made goodness, or our virtues, or even our own hard work. Rather, it is because of this inner goodness that somebody else has loved us first—significant others in our life, and ultimately God himself. The unbreakable covenant whereby God has joined himself to us in love is the outstanding scriptural symbol that calls us to open ourselves to receive his love and to trust in it: "Though the mountains leave their place and the hills be shaken, my love shall never leave you . . ., says the Lord who has mercy on you" (Isa. 54:10).

The scriptural message indicates that we are good and worthy of affirmation not because of anything we have accomplished but simply because we *are*. Our existence is not an accident; there are no illegitimate persons in God's plan. We are a special creation of the One in whose image we were made. Saint Paul insists that we have been "chosen" by God. On the day of our baptism we believe we are joined so intimately with Christ that the Father regards us precisely as his own Son on the day of his baptism: "You are my beloved, in whom I am well pleased" (Luke 3:22). In a word, the Scriptures are always warning us against putting ultimate trust in our own works. They ask us simply to accept the free, gracious action of God calling us into being and saying, "You are good!" "You are wonderful." That is why I find a lot of meaning in infant baptism. A helpless child, having accomplished nothing in life, is told by everyone, including God, how wonderful it is. Let us repeat the steps of affirmation:

1. You exist.
2. It is good that you exist.
3. It is good that you *do*.

A small book which I recommend to all my clients and students, *Poverty of Spirit*, by Father Johannes B. Metz, points to the necessity of affirmation in relationship to self:

> Man's self-acceptance is the basis of the Christian creed. Assent to God starts in man's sincere assent to himself, just as sinful flight from God starts in man's flight from himself. In accepting the chalice of his existence, man shows his obedience to the will of his Father in heaven (cfr. Mt. 26, 39, 42): in rejecting it, he rejects God.

Knowing the temptation which Humanity itself is, knowing how readily man tries to escape the harsh distress of the human situation, knowing how difficult it is for him to bear with himself and how quickly he feels betrayed by himself, knowing how difficult it is for man not to hate himself (as Bernanos points out), we can then understand why God had to prescribe "self-love" as a virtue and one of the great commandments. We can then understand why we constantly need the help of His grace. We can then realize how much easier it is to say "no" instead of "yes" to oneself, and why all asceticism is first designed to serve this great "yes."[8]

Self-Affirmation

Notice that I am not advocating self-affirmation. In fact, there is just too much self-this and self-that around today, for example, self-actualization, self-realization, self-fulfillment, self-gratification, and even spiritual self-direction.[9] All these "selfs" seem to say that the whole world depends on me and I totally upon myself. Self-affirmation is always futile because it places the emphasis on things, power, and control rather than on open receptiveness to the love of another human being.

Loving Yourself is not Selfishness

Jesus emphasized love of self as next in importance to loving God: "You shall love your neighbor as yourself" (Matt. 22:39, Mark 12:31, Luke 10:27). Note the Evangelists do not tell us, "Love your neighbor *instead* of

8. Johannes B. Metz, *Poverty of Spirit*, (New York: Paulist Press, 1968), p. 7.

9. Paul C. Vitz, *Psychology As Religion: The Cult of Self-Worship,* (Grand Rapids, MI: Eerdmans Pubishing Co., 1977), p. 29.

yourself.'' Proper love of self is thus the prerequisite and criterion for our behavior toward our neighbor.

Many people become nervous and uncomfortable when we speak of affirmation in reference to self because of the fear of being egotistical or selfish. Selfish love is well illustrated by the Greek myth of Narcissus. This youth fell in love with his own reflection in a well, and, totally engrossed with his own image, tumbled into the water and drowned. From this myth the word narcissism is derived. Selfish persons, like Narcissus, are engrossed with themselves and become egotistical. Walter Trobisck put it bluntly when he wrote that ''whoever does not love himself is an egoist.'' Persons who do not love themselves become egoists out of necessity; they are not sure of their identity and therefore are always trying to find themselves.

Thomas Aquinas

In our efforts to become humble we have allowed the self-denial philosophy to negate proper self-love. ''The highest form of friendship can be likened to self-love. . . . A friend is loved as one for whom we desire something; and man also loves himself in exactly the same way.'' For Thomas Aquinas, friendship is the image and self-love the original; we love our friends as we love ourselves.

Introspection

Let us turn to the theme of self-knowledge and understanding. Through the centuries humanity has been aware of its need to know more about its inner world but has found it extremely difficult to look inside itself. The frustrations encountered in this process of introspection have been expressed: "The heart of man is a stubborn thing, full of tears; who shall fathom it?" or "No one ever knows whether one has really been able to penetrate into all the secret places of the heart." (In classical writings, heart is often used interchangeably to mean mind.) The great church fathers from Augustine to Aquinas were even humbler in their claims to human knowledge.

Earlier in history we find the wise men of those days telling their people to find out more about themselves. The oracles of ancient Greece contained the motto, "Know thyself." The psalmist phrased the same thought in the form of a question when he said, "What is man that thou art mindful of him?" (Ps. 8:5). In more recent years this sentiment was expressed vividly in the words of the Scottish poet "Bobby" Burns, "Oh, wad some power the giftie gie us, to see oursels as others see us!" Through the centuries, then, people have longed to know more about the way they function.

The process of introspection is an interesting phenomenon. Finding out about oneself is at first a very natural event. It begins shortly after birth. A child, a unique being, is placed in the midst of a mysterious world with which sooner or later it must come to terms. Instinctively curious, the child begins to explore its world and itself, fingering objects as well as its body. The child very soon gains a concept of what it is like. Have you ever watched a baby in a crib playing with its toes and putting them in its mouth? The infant is saying to itself, as it were, "This is I. This is what I am like."

The Big Me

When the child is a bit older, parents assist it in this self-knowledge when they ask it to point to its eyes, its nose, its mouth, and so on. In this way it develops a concept of its body and then differentiates it from others around it. "You are daddy, this is sister, that is a dog," and so on. After the child knows itself physically, it experiences itself as a social being. It exists in relationship to others. It experiences itself as a person who can be manipulated or who can manipulate others in order to get things accomplished. The infant receives constant attention from its parents. It is the central figure of the family world. Its world is a self-centered one in which it is what I call "the big me."

As the child grows, however, and learns that there are others around with whom it must share and whom it must consider, its "big me" becomes smaller and smaller. The "big me" or self-centeredness yields to the "little me" or selflessness. On the one hand we have selfishness—on the other, selflessness. Through the ongoing process of maturation and through the emotional security derived from affirming parents the child develops into adulthood where the individual "puts away childish things," the cloak of personal selfishness. The process is slow and at times painful. But people are mature when they have developed the capacity within themselves to deny or sacrifice personal pleasure in order to live beyond their own little world through the lives and activities of others.

Be Careful

A word of warning is necessary here. I often see clients who carry the practice of introspection too far. They look at every variable, read motives into every action; sometimes they appear to think they can control their entire environment. They are like jugglers trying to catch every ball. Introspection which leads to self-knowledge, which in turn allows insights to change behavior, is affirming to the self and others. Introspection which is carried on in a scrupulous manner becomes futile and depressing and, more often than not, promotes a self-centered and narcissistic outlook on life.

Felt Goodness

Basically we all need to be able to say, "I feel very good about myself as a human being." This has nothing to do with what we have done or how intelligent we are or how successful we seem to have been in our life. Again, this is not an intellectual abstraction. It is a *feeling*. Sometimes we know a fact intellectually, but in our heart of hearts we do not really believe it, or perhaps, realize it. I can think of many people whom I have met in the course of my travels who have said to me, "Yes, I know I am good, but I don't feel it."

Feeling good and knowing that I am good can come only through the relationships I invite into my life. An affirming relationship with the significant other is the most important factor which will allow us to feel as well as know that we are, indeed, creatures of a beneficent creator. We are good because God made us good, unconditionally. If we accept that we have been made in the divine image and allow other persons to affirm this image, with all the beauty, marvel, and mystery that this process implies, then we will be affirmed in proper self-love.

Affirmation is Relationship with God

We cannot affirm God in the sense that we have thus far been using the word affirmation, that is, to make strong, to make firm, or to give strength to. We can add nothing to God's existence. What we can do in reference to God is to allow him time and space in our lives so that we can receive his affirmation of us. Over one hundred times a year the Church prays a part of the Mass called the ordinary preface which declares: "You have no need of our praise, but our praise itself becomes your gift to us." We open ourselves to God's affirmation of our goodness and we praise him. We must learn to listen to God, for he speaks softly: through a sign, a look, a touch, a thought, an event, and other people. As we become more attentive, we will perceive more readily what he has to say. We must remember, however, that the journey to God does not mean getting lost in an extraordinary or spectacular moment of experiencing God. It is a process of encountering myself and God in the everydayness of life.

Understanding God

Obviously, you cannot allow God to affirm you if you do not grow in understanding of God and his revelation of love in the person of Jesus of Nazareth. J. B. Phillip lists several misconceptions about God in his book *Your God Is Too Small*, naming them, among others, Resident Policeman, Grand Old Man, Meek and Mild, The God of One Hundred Percent, Heavenly Bosom, and God-in-a-Box. In his book, *God's Will Is Not Lost*, John MacArthur notes that many people are afraid of God because they truly believe that he is a kind of "cosmic killjoy, stomping on everyone's fun and raining on parades.'' The point is that if our concept of God is inaccurate or incomplete, we limit God's affirmation of us.

Spiritual and Psychic Patterns

Our spiritual lives and relationship with God generally follow the pattern of our psychic structure. Persons who attempt to compensate for insecurity through achievement will exhibit that same dynamic in their spiritual life. It is not uncommon to see people who appear to be trying to prove to God that they are good. Their image of God is one of a stern taskmaster who is never satisfied or pleased. The reality is, of course, that their own critical observing selves are never satisfied. Another form of spiritualization that is a compensation for a low sense of personal worth is to make God the sole and exclusive affirmer. In this situation, God becomes the substitute for affirming human relationships. Perhaps nobody else loves me, but I know that at least God does. I know my life matters to him, and I can hang on to this truth when all else fails. This form of spirituality will fail in time because it is founded on an intellctualized truth rather than felt experience. It is simply another form of talking oneself into good feelings. It is like the abandoned child telling herself that she knows her parents love her even though they left her and have not returned.

Jesus Christ

God's plan from the beginning of time was that ultimately the complete fullness of affirmation is to be found in and through Christ. "Before the world was made, he chose us, chose us in Christ, to be holy and blameless, and to live in love in his presence, determined that we should become his adopted children through Jesus Christ" (Eph. 1:3-4). Jesus is God's divine-human affirmation of humanity and he is at the same time our "amen" to God. The New Testament does not look to Jesus merely for a solution to the problems of humanity. It encourages us to look through Christ to the Godhead. Christ's central moral exhortation was that people must love God and one another. Through this idea he was revealing to us the nature of God and humanity. The importance of Jesus was not only what he was in himself, perfect man, but that he was the Word of God, an explanation of God to humanity.

The image of Christ working among people and involved in the human situation is so compelling that it is easy to forget that this man is God. Christ exemplifies perfectly a mature sense of identity: "The Father is in Me and I in the Father" (John 4:34).

The identity of a person of faith is contained in the will of God, in the ideal that God wishes that person to attain. This model is often hidden and is only gradually revealed. In each instance, this ideal is simply Christ under a new aspect.

Faith

Affirmation by God and affirmation of humanity provide the only solution to the riddle of life. The alternatives seen in the life of the nonaffirmed are a meaningless, inhuman functionalism, hectic flight, and self-centered pride. To be open to affirmation demands faith, which is a gift of the Father. Faith means partaking in God's life and is a freely given grace from God. Faith means to say yes to

God's revelation. It is God's view of reality; to see with the eyes of faith is to see with the eyes of God.

As Paul points out:

> Of this wisdom it is written: "No eye has seen, nor ear heard, nor the heart of man conceived, what God has prepared for those who love him."
>
> God has revealed this wisdom to us through the Spirit. For the Spirit searches everything, even the depths of God. For what person knows a man's thoughts except the spirit of the man which is in him? So also no one comprehends the thoughts of God except the Spirit of God. Now we have received not the spirit of the world, but the Spirit which is from God, that we might understand the gifts bestowed on us by God. And we impart this in words not taught by human wisdom but taught by the Spirit, interpreting spiritual truths to those who possess the Spirit.
>
> The unspiritual man does not receive the gifts of the Spirit of God, for they are folly to him, and he is not able to understand them because they are spiritually discerned. The spiritual man judges all things, but is himself to be judged by no one. For "who has known the mind of the Lord so as to instruct him?" But we have the mind of Christ (1 Cor. 2:9-16).

Signs

The signs of God's affirmation are many: in creation, in his relationship with Christ and his Church, and in the sacraments, dogmas, prayers, and other elements of faith. All these signs indicate that when God's love is revealed in Christ there is really no limit to his divine love. It transcends all our human thoughts. God's affirmation and fidelity are emphasized in the infinite love of Jesus Christ for humanity. That Christ loves us is the great secret, the most intimate secret of every soul. It is the most inconceivable reality; yet it is a reality which would completely change our lives if we could but realize it fully. This realization requires not merely a theoretical knowledge of this mystery as a revealed truth, but an awareness of this love similar to our awareness of the love of a beloved. It also implies an awareness of the incomparable, unique character of this divine love, its absolutely new and mysterious quality, and its ineffable holiness, as it shines forth in the gospel and the liturgy and is mirrored in the lives of the saints.

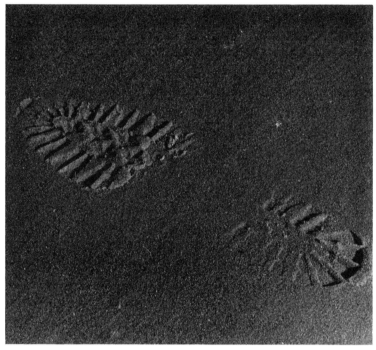

Having been affirmed by another and affirming others, you will know and feel who you are; you will have a true identity. You will sense that you are different but acceptable, that you not only belong in the world but that you are contributing to it and can change it; that there is a unique place for you and that you have a unique contribution; that you can choose freely to love and to do, and that you cannot be ultimately destroyed. You can be confidently open to the future.

—Thomas A. Kane

Chapter V

The Obstacles to Affirmation

Life is like an onion.
You take off one layer at a time,
and sometimes you cry.

—Carl Sandburg

When we speak about the process of affirmation, it may appear that all people grow in affirmation in the same way and manner. Such an assumption is not true. During the maturation of the adolescent or adult, there may be significant obstacles to giving affirmation resulting from individual experiences and influences. If we know about these obstacles, we can recognize their effect in our own lives and the lives of others, and our expectations will conform much more to reality. The obstacles to affirmation are:

1. an early life experience of nonaffirmation;
2. a teaching that the emotions are bad;
3. an image of the self that is idealized.

An Early Life Experience of Nonaffirmation

As babies grow older and more active, their means of communication multiply. They begin to walk, to reach out, to seek out others, to respond to the human voice, and to use their own voice in a more expressive way. They gesture, protest, gurgle, and express delight. Their command of language develops.

Simple sounds, such as "ma-ma" and "da-da," come to have a special and personal meaning. Mother is not only a person who gives to the child; she is now identified with a verbal symbol. The child's reactions to the mother are not always positive and, according to the circumstances, anxiety or anger may be the result of the communication between the two. This discord happens, for example, when the mother in her wisdom does not yield to all of the child's demands.

By the end of the second year, verbal communication assumes increasing importance. The child acquires skill in forming phrases and sentences which have meaning. Words come to have social and private meanings. One often sees preschool children talking to imaginary people and excluding their parents and others from the conversation. This type of private, fantasy-filled communication is given up when the child's enlarging world of school and peers engages its interest.

During this phase, the child frequently does not want to give up childish gratifications in the face of difficulties. This behaviour is especially apparent when a new brother or sister comes along and temporarily threatens the child's position in the family hierarchy. During such periods of tension the parents must convey to the child some idea of its continued importance and their acceptance of it. Only with feelings of being affirmed will the child's concepts of self-worth emerge so it can go on to further phases of growth and development.

Identification

The main psychological mechanism by which the child accomplishes this growth is called identification. If the child were able to explain this process logically, which of course it cannot do, it would reason somewhat in this manner: "To be like my parents is to be loved" or "I will be accepted by them (my parents) if I am like them."

This attitude implies identification with a more powerful person. In the child's mind, the parent is larger, stronger, and more capable than it is. Since the child is smaller, weaker, and quite dependent upon its parents, it follows what is in effect the adult concept of, "If you can't lick them—join them." In order to feel more secure, the child tries in every possible way to imitate or mimic the thoughts, feelings, and actions of its parents or any other adult upon whom it is dependent or from whom it wants respect and affirmation.

From school age through adolescence and indeed even in adulthood, individuals struggle for personal identity. They borrow from the strength or weaknesses of all those with whom they come in contact: their parents, friends, teachers, clergy, employers. More and more, then, as the child relates to others, it develops its own distinct social personality and appreciates itself as an individual, separate and unique from its parents. Nevertheless, the child continues to carry with it many of their qualities, precepts, and social values which become in effect its standards for living.

Don't Pass the Buck

What and how we learned as children may have a profound effect on our present life. I do not suggest that "passing the buck" or blaming everything on childhood is the answer to free and autonomous living. Frequently, I encounter clients who are hesitant to explore their early childhood development, their feelings about their mother, father, or siblings. They protest that these experiences are in the past, that nothing is to be gained by recrimination, and that parents are not to blame. Yet daily they suffer the torment of nonaffirmation and the deep perception that they do not measure up. They are unable to allow another person to affirm them. Such persons often portray their family as near perfect. They cannot bring themselves to acknowledge their parents' faults because they would have to come to terms with their own lack of perfection.

Often these same persons freely blame church or religious authorities for their troubled present. They have an insatiable need for their superiors as well as for themselves to be perfect. This need is a perpetuation of an insidious cycle of self-destruction and inhuman self-rejection.

Frequently neurotic guilt leads us to perceive ourselves as victims of the past, of parents, of institutions, and of people who represent those institutions. We see it as their fault that we feel helpless, hopeless, or injured. Indeed, there may be some truth to this feeling. However, blame will satisfy us for only a short time; it will not really make us feel better.[1]

When we blame, we engage in a process called projection. Our inadequacy is placed on some other person or on the environment. Basically we avoid personal responsibility. Jung writes:

> Only the living presence of the eternal images can lead the human psyche to a dignity which makes it morally possible for a man to stand by his own soul, and be convinced that it is worth his while to persevere with it. Only then will he realize that the conflict is in him, that the discord and tribulation are his riches, which should not be squandered by attacking others: and that, if fate should exact a debt from him in the form of guilt it is a debt to himself. Then he will recognize the worth of his psyche, for nobody can owe a debt to a mere nothing.[2]

There is no need to blame anyone. We can accept personal responsibility for all the feelings we experience. They are not necessarily destructive and may lead to an awareness that we are people limited by time, influenced by culture, and living in a present historical moment.

Behaviorism

As we discussed earlier, an early life experience of non-affirmation is an obstacle to affirmation. We have seen that often an individual is limited because as a child there was little or no love shown. Many parents of the thirties,

---

1. E. J. Franasiak, "When Enough Is Not Enough: Affirmed Sufficiency and Guilt," in *Guilt*, Kathleen E. Kelley, ed., (Whitinsville, MA:, Affirmation Books, 1980), p. 141.

2. Carl G. Jung, *Collected Works,* vol. 14 (Princeton, NJ: Princeton University Press, 1959), pp. 363-64.

forties, and fifties were very influenced by a school of psychology called behaviorism. The echoes of its damaging effects are still evident in the eighties.

In order to understand the behaviorist school of thought fully, consider this statement by John B. Watson, its founder:

> Mothers just don't know, when they kiss their children and pick them up and rock them, caress them and jiggle them upon their knee, that they are slowly building up a human being totally unable to cope with the world it must later live in. . . . There is a sensible way of treating children. Treat them as though they were young adults. . . . Never hug or kiss them, never let them sit on your lap. If you must, kiss them on the forehead when they say goodnight. . . . Can't a mother train herself to substitute a kindly word, a smile, in all her dealings with the child, for the kiss and the hug, the pickup and the coddlings? . . . If you haven't a nurse and cannot leave the child, put it out in the back yard a large part of the day. Build a fence around the yard so that you are sure no harm can come to it. Do this from the time it is born. . . . If your heart is too tender and you must watch the child, make yourself a peephole so that you can see it without being seen, or use a periscope. . . . Finally, learn not to talk in endearing and coddling terms.[3]

Many parents who are horrified by such an approach to childrearing have done irreparable harm to their children in a thousand other ways: by alternating between overpermissiveness and punitiveness, by excessive criticism, and so on. Most of us, in fact, have had an experience of nonaffirmation in childhood, by well-meaning parents who firmly believed they loved us, yet who failed to display

3. John B. Watson, *Psychological Care of the Infant and Child* (New York: Norton Company, 1928), p. 16.

that love in the simplest and most fundamental ways: by touching and cuddling, by praise and affirmation.

A Teaching that the Emotions are Bad

There is a tragic stream in the social history of Christianity that seems to maintain that the emotions are bad. This attitude is very unfortunate because the authentic Christian teaching speaks, in fact, about the nobility of emotions. Not many years ago one of the most insulting things you could say to a person was "You're too emotional." My Jesuit colleague, Father Bernard Bush, tells of a Jesuit adage which was repeated with pride: "Jesuits meet without affection, live in silence, and part without regret." The intellectual powers were considered to be the highest and noblest parts of the soul, and much time was spent in cultivating them. The effect of such training on many priests and religious, and directly or indirectly on the laity, was often devastating. Somehow, what was going on deep inside of people in the form of love, anger, depression, joy, sorrow, loneliness, and so forth, did not seem to have much connection to the spiritual life.

Positive Attitude Needed

Before anything constructive can be done to integrate emotional development with spiritual growth, a longstanding attitude of rejection of the emotions has to be changed. We need today a rethinking of spiritual writings and a reinterpretation of them in the light of what is now known about the normal functioning of the human personality.[4] Because emotional reactions can and frequently do

---

4. Some of the most valuable current contributions in this area of concern are the books and essays of Adrian Van Kaam of Duquesne University.

hinder rational control, the emotions have been unfavorably regarded by Westerners ever since the flowering of intellectual life in the Golden Age of Greek philosophy. At times this negative attitude has taken the form of complete suppression, as in classical Stoicism. At other times it has flared into open hostility, as in Manichaeanism.

History affords many examples which show that this negative and repressive attitude toward emotion is not merely the result of misguided tendencies in Christian asceticism. But it is no less clear that Christianity, even with the central doctrine of the Incarnation to guide it, did little to neutralize this intolerant attitude toward human emotion. During certain periods this intolerance has appeared in the Church in extreme form. Yet, despite clear condemnation of these excesses, this tendency to exalt reason at the expense of emotion is still with us.

As long as the emotions are regarded as foiling humanity's efforts to grow in holiness, the integration of emotional and spiritual development will not come about. Indeed, we might rather wish that the emotions would not develop at all. But if we are serious about trying to develop this integration, we must delete from our personal principles such convenient and time-honored half-truths as "love of God has nothing to do with feeling. It is a matter of the will."

Now, it is quite clear that a love of God that consists of feeling or emotion alone is not worthy of the name; but neither is there such a thing as a love of God that is purely intellectual.[5] There is no sanction in scripture for this exaltation of the rational and intellectual at the expense of the affective life. Even wisdom, which is so generously extolled in the inspired books, is rather the understanding heart or knowledge of God that carries with it total commitment to his divine plan. The intemperate adulation of intellect or reason betrays pagan contamination, not the authentic Judeo-Christian tradition. Moreover, it reflects an image of a human being that is philosophically unsound and psychologically misleading.

Each of us is a psychosomatic unit, and any attempt at asceticism or spiritual advancement at the expense of this unity is doomed to failure. We might have hoped that the full acceptance of the Incarnation and the pursuit of a thoroughly Christocentric spirituality would have eliminated such erroneous attitudes, but such is far from the case. The emotional sensitivity and unfailing empathy of Christ are experienced by all who know him. Even his emphatic reiteration of the first precept of the decalogue, "You shall love the Lord your God with your whole heart and your whole soul and your whole mind," might have saved Christian asceticism from contamination by the errors of pagan rationalism, but, unfortunately, it did not.

All Emotions are Good

Sometimes when I visit a seminary or religious house, I see signs or banners proclaiming "Love," "Joy," "Peace," and I wonder why there are none extolling "Sadness,"

5. Karol Wojtyla (John Paul II), "Christ fully reveals man to man himself," *Sign of Contradiction* (St. Paul Publications, London, 1979), p. 101.

"Loneliness," or at least a sign about struggle and pilgrimage. There is no emotion that is bad. All emotions are good!

Yes, all emotions are good! They are not neutral or bad in themselves. God created our emotions to help us live richly and fully.

All emotions tell us something about ourselves. Joy tells us something; but so does anger. We must be comfortable about being feeling persons and not be frightened or thrown into panic because of what is primary and most natural to humanity: that the human person has emotions. Once we declare that all our feelings are good and become emotionally comfortable with this human reality, we have the opportunity to grow in affirmation and be affirmed and affirming individuals.

Comfortable and Uncomfortable Feelings

Once known and allowed to be, feelings can help us to keep life situations in proportion and to grow emotionally. Some feelings are comfortable, for example, joy, trust, happiness; and some may be uncomfortable, for example, anger, hate, sadness. But regardless of whether they are comfortable or not, feelings when governed by reason contribute to our personalities. It is important that we not ignore or repress our feelings. If we try to escape from our feelings or to live as if they have nothing to do with our personalities, then we are putting ourselves in a dangerous position. It is vital that the young be properly educated about the role emotions play in their lives, so that they do not grow into adulthood trying to ignore feelings or living in a state of guilt about something ordinarily so beautiful and so nobly creative.

Life is Emotions

Emotions are energetic mobilizations of the body which reveal or transform the world in a certain way and which seek to be shared with other people. Though it is evident that differences in strength and kind of emotions exist, it does not seem possible to discriminate clearly the emotional from other aspects of life. It seems, in fact, that emotions are coextensive with life itself. And this is actually so, for the individual's life is emotion. We breathe (move and live) and our breathing reflects our emotional state. If I am anxious, breathing momentarily stops and is shallow and quick. In anger, breathing is deep and labored, forced through tightened muscles. In joy, breathing is deep, easy, and complete. In depression, breathing is shallow and slow, accompanied with an occasional sigh. Breath, as indicated in Genesis, stands for life itself: "God breathed life into him" (Gen. 2:7). Breathing and breath are inextricably tied to being emotional, for to be alive and breathing means to-be-able-to-move and to-be-able-to-be-moved. Having a body which is alive always means to have a certain bodily tone or mood, to perceive reality in a specific light, and to move toward sharing with others. Emotions are the life within me, or the movement that I am as a living creature. This is not to say that a person is only emotional but rather that a person's life or the force of movement in the person is emotion. To be fully human means to be movable and to be fully immovable means to be dead.

However, being alive or dead is not a question of either/or. Sometimes a person is more alive (more lively, spirited, moved, and movable) than at other times. In fact, it is fairly easy to characterize people according to their general degree of liveliness. This liveliness is much influenced by the attitude a person has learned toward emotions. Our culture's fundamental ambivalence in regard to emotionality is reflected in our valuation of liveliness. Particularly within middle-class Christian culture, liveliness and enthusiasm along with other strong feelings are often viewed with a certain disfavor. Persons influenced by this attitude tend to dampen not only their uncomfortable feelings, but their strongly comfortable feelings as well. Negative evaluations are held not only of anger and sexual feelings, but also of religious impulses and ecstasy. Every variation of emotion is supposed to be cooled off and moderated: "You mustn't get carried away, you know." For example, even today we see some people reacting disapprovingly toward the sign of peace, usually a handshake, in the liturgy. This negative attitude toward emotionality has rather serious consequences religiously as well as socially, for religious and human life are by implication condemned to a half-life of moderation. Such an attitude goes directly against the most fundamental Christian tradition. Christian faith is intended to be an invitation to abundant life.

Christians who live in fear of their emotions in a fundamental sense choose death rather than life. This choice is usually not totally effective (except in suicide), for life (motion and emotion) is stronger than mere will and cannot be chosen out of existence. Nevertheless, to see emotion as something primarily to be curbed, held back, suppressed, and repressed is to call life itself a dark, evil, and demonic force. The tangible result of viewing emotions as demonic is often a mousey, unlively, and uninspired existence of timorous caution. For those who are called to be "fools for Christ," this attitude is most bizarre.

When emotions are seen within a humanly meaningful context as reliable beacons in our life together, it is possible for them to become what they intrinsically are: a certain light on the world, given in the moving body and tending toward being shared with others. Within this view emotions are already seen as connected with reality, as it is our emotions which open up the world. Taking such a stand toward emotions can liberate the forces or energy of the person and make possible affirmation in religious and social life. Affirmation is not something merely added on to the emotional life of humanity; it is rather the appropriate fulfillment of emotionality, of the movement of life within a person toward relationship with other human beings and with God.

An Image of the Self that is Idealized

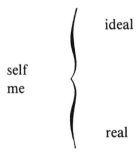

self
me

ideal

real

The Ideal Self

The third and most serious obstacle to affirmation is an idealized image of self. All of us have ideals; we want to develop our potential, to become the person we feel we can be. We know we are incomplete, that we sometimes fail and need forgiveness. But we see life as a journey toward God, and we see ourselves as always growing in grace as we travel on our pilgrimage. What makes this attitude healthy is our realistic image of self. We know our gifts, and we accept our failings.

But persons with an idealized self-image are not gentle with themselves. They are compulsive in their struggle toward self-realization, and they have an unrealistic vision of the self to which they wish to conform. They want to attain the glory of this ideal self quickly, not through a natural process of growth. They expect to mold themselves to this image without prolonged effort, and they do not recognize that they have limitations which are incompatible with their ideal. Their imagination aids them in distorting the truth. They have difficulty distinguishing between genuine feelings, beliefs, and strivings, and the artificial equivalents in themselves and others. For them the emphasis is on appearing rather than on being.

Sometimes this problem begins early in life when the child is expected to conform to the parental ideal of what a son or daughter should be. When young people enter religious or seminary life, they are again presented with an idealized image of the model priest, sister, or brother. Married couples sometimes assume they must live up to the idealized role of the perfect wife or husband. In all these cases the individuals eventually realize, "I'm not perfect. I'm not the ideal. I have faults." If they cannot learn as they mature to live with their limitations and weaknesses, they will find themselves living a compulsive life of "I should" and "I must," no matter how unrealistic their expectations may be. The more the unconscious drive to actualize their idealized self dominates their life, the more these inner dictates become the sole moving force of life. Life becomes very complicated, because these persons not only apply the standards of "I should" and "I must" to their own lives, but to the behavior of the people with whom they live and work. They set up the same impossible goals for those around them. Part of the problem is that these ideals are actually impossible to fulfill. These troubled persons ignore the actual conditions that exist and the abilities and characteristics of the individuals involved. Such false expectations can be distinguished from realistic ideals because the persons who hold these expectations assume they will be fulfilled without real effort, and they deny themselves and others spontaneity and the freedom of choice.

How can you recognize this behavior in yourself or others? You are unrealistic if you assume rights which others do not have. If you consider yourself an exception, if you claim to be exempt from laws, rules, necessities, and restrictions, so that you expect life to be easy for you, free from illness, and successful without effort on your part, you are unrealistic. You are demanding that reality be adjusted to your own needs, regardless of the needs or rights of others. Some people, if they are honest, will admit that they feel things are owed to them without their making adequate effort. They expect to lose weight without dieting. If they are lonely, they wait for someone to call them. This attitude is rooted in the refusal to accept responsibility. Then when these people see they are not identical with their ideal self, they can blame forces outside themselves for their failure.

A good example of an idealized image would be the "perfect" religious who never says no to any task she is asked to do, even if it means working forty-eight hours in a twenty-four-hour day. The ideal priest is never distracted in prayer. The ideal mother is always patient. What happens to people who try to live as their idealized self-images? When they reach middle age and they begin to realize they are not the ideal person they had been assuming they were, they commence to hate the real person. I hear this from clients over and over again. "I hate the real me. If other people knew the real me, they would hate me, too." The ideal self says, "I will be God. I will control my life. Everything will conform to my expectations." In a sense, these people have experienced a grave injustice in being presented with only the ideal. A life lived this way is a tragic one.

Jesus did not always conform to the ideal image of a teacher that others had. He did not always give the ideal response. When the woman taken in adultery was brought to him, the teachers of the law and the Pharisees expected Christ to condemn her as they did. Who could forgive her or make her strong or firm? She did not fulfill the ideal. She was a real person. The law said to stone her. But Jesus saw the goodness of the woman and responded in a gentle and affirming way. There is something of the adulteress in each one of us, in the real person that we are. We have only the real me to live with, the one person that we are. We admit we need conversion and growth, but we must live with the real person. There is no one else.

If we have always struggled to become our idealized self, then our real self never had a chance to develop. We find we cannot reach the ideal and we cannot live with our real self. We need to become conscious of how we have internalized our idealized self because this whole realm of reality sometimes stays in the unconscious. We find ourselves saying, "I can't do anything. I cannot live with my shortcomings. I hate myself." Living this way is especially difficult if we suffer from excessive compulsion neurosis. We get into obsessional patterns and worry about them. We live with fear. "I must," "I should," "I have to" live up to the great expectations that the ideal self imposes upon my life. We tend to become rigid and inflexible. We need to realize that there is only one creator. We are the created ones, and we live in the real world, the world of the adult, the world of pilgrimage, the world of struggle. It is also the world of peace and joy, but not the childish world where everything is fitted around our expectations. That self-centeredness is the sin of Adam all over again. "I will have power over everyone and everything. There will be no imperfection." This attitude is a great obstacle to affirming others and forming relationships with them. What we find many times in the life of movements and congregations and people who perpetuate the ideal notion is a perverted sense of self-glorification.

The Real Self

On the other hand, if we live with the real self we are caught up with the idea of God's mercy, and we abandon ourselves to that mercy. We must get in touch with the real person, not just the spiritual part which needs prayer, but the physical which needs rest, and the emotional which needs leisure. When ideals are presented to us by ourselves or others, we stay in touch with the real person while we consider them and choose the ones that are possible for us to work toward realistically. Karen Horney speaks of the real self as "that central inner force, common to all human beings and yet unique in each, which is the deep source of growth."[6] The real self includes the innate gifts, potential, and limitations of the person; it also comprises the person's feelings, capacity to express them, willpower, and ability to make decisions and relate to others. The real self is the person's "basic inner reality; the actual feelings, wishes, thoughts, memories, and fantasies . . . as these arise spontaneously."[7] The real self is not static. It goes through a process of change, a course of evolution as growth takes place in the individual. According to Horney, the real self is the "original force toward individual growth and fulfillment."[8]

Personality integration is possible only when persons are in touch with their real selves. When individuals are in touch with their spontaneous feelings so that they are able to make decisions, be responsible for them, and accept their consequences, such persons manifest an integrated and authentic identity.

We can strive for our ideals in the process of growth, but we must live at the same time with our incompleteness. What is that real self? It is made up of me in all my dimensions. I accept myself physically: my looks, my height and weight, my so-called flaws. I accept myself emotionally,

6. Karen Horney, M.D., *Neurosis and Human Growth* (New York: W. W. Norton, 1950), p. 17.
7. Ibid.
8. Ibid.

spiritually, intellectually: with my gifts and skills or my apparent lack of them. Part of the conversion experience psychically and spiritually is to live in the world of the real me. Saint Therese of Lisieux expressed this beautifully: "If you are willing to bear serenely the trial of being displeasing to yourself, you will be to Jesus a pleasant place of shelter."

It is true that sin, the deliberate choice of evil, can keep us away from Jesus, but our imperfections will not hinder us. Saying that we are going to be perfect will keep us away from the Good Shepherd. The Church suffered through that heresy when people received the Eucharist only when they felt worthy. Who of us is ever worthy to be united with Christ? When we live in the real world we live a life of limitations—emotionally, intellectually, physically, spiritually. I may have to refuse a task because I cannot physically or emotionally take on another duty. If I cannot say no, then I am not really free to say yes. If I have said yes throughout my life, and never no, then I have never really said yes. I must be free to choose my response. The beauty of vocation is that I can say no as well as yes. If sometimes we are not happy with our answer, we can learn and grow from the experience.

I am saddened when I remember an elderly sister who could not accept her imperfections. She never felt that she had lived the religious life well, because she had experienced involuntary feelings of jealousy all through her life. Yet Paul speaks of the thorn in his flesh that was given to him to keep him humble. In a sense that sister could have looked on her weakness as Paul did his.

We must surrender ourselves as we are to God. Therapists are not spiritual directors; we do not need to tell our clients who the real me is. They can discover that for themselves. We therapists have sincere feelings for our clients. We observe them fighting for their real lives. It is interesting to see at the beginning of therapy how sure clients are that they will not be able to work things through and then to watch their progress as they learn to know and accept themselves.

This freedom of choice to say yes or no is important in our lives. Few of us believe in determinism. When I hear therapists talking about the psychology of determinism, I wonder why they take anyone in therapy. If human beings are determined in their behavior, then what good will insights do them?

American literature has numerous examples of tragic characters who do not accept their limitations and who try to fulfill their ideal image. In Edwin O'Connor's *The Edge of Sadness*, Father Hugh Kennedy comes to realize that he has spent years immersed in the duties that he thought he should perform as the ideal priest. Upon seeing that he was mistaken in what he considered most important, he slips into depression and alcoholism. In *Death of a Salesman* by Arthur Miller, Willy Lohman collapses completely when his idealized image of himself as a supersalesman is shattered.

The pride of the angels, of Adam, of the Israelites in the desert, is the same pride behind the idealized self. It is an arrogant position that leads some persons to avoid a life of service in relationship to others. But it is the real me who lives in community; it is the real others that I see in community. If I am living with or dealing with people who have this idealized self-image, I can try to understand them and our relationship. I may be able to recognize when they are trying to change their behavior, which is extremely difficult, and I can support them as they attempt to start living in the real world.

Vulnerability

When we consider the obstacles to affirmation whether in ourselves or in others, we come close to understanding something about vulnerability. Affirmation always involves vulnerability. When we open ourselves and permit another person to know that we love that individual, we risk being hurt. Because we all are to some extent nonaffirmed, we know how it feels to be hurt, and this risk is frightening.

Everyone has probably felt at times like the woman in the throes of marital problems who says, "I don't ever want to care for anyone that much again! It just hurts too much." The vulnerability of the affirmer is inescapable in every sphere of human relationship. If some tragic misfortune occurs and a child in our family is killed or seriously injured, we suffer deeply, much more than if it were a child down the street whom we scarcely know.

On a somewhat less intense level, schoolteachers care for the children in their classrooms. Their affirmation has its satisfactions, but there are also hurts when some children seem unwilling or unable to respond to the teacher's interest in them and their welfare.

So striking is the relationship between affirmation and vulnerability that it can almost be stated mathematically. The closer we are emotionally to another human being and the more clearly we express our caring, the more open we are to the possibility of being hurt by that person and the more intensely we will feel the hurt. It is this possibility that frightens us and keeps us wary about establishing close relationships.

We will probably experience some of the hurt that we fear when we risk love. If we establish significant and close relationships, we will sometimes be saddened by those we affirm. If we share confidences, we will occasionally be betrayed. If we count on people, they will sometimes let us down. If we express warmth, others will at times seem indifferent or even cold.

It works the other way, too, of course. It is inevitable that we will sometimes hurt those who affirm us, even though we love them. Sometimes we will be fully aware of what we are doing and yet seem unable to stop ourselves. At other times we will not realize, at the moment at least, that we are inflicting hurt.

The Futile "Flight" of the Nonaffirmed

1. flight into bullying or bragging

2. flight into attempting to win acceptance

3. flight into delinquent behavior

4. flight into utopian world

5. flight into physical symptoms or illness

6. flight into emotional illness

7. flight into alcoholism or other drug addiction

8. flight into overeating

9. flight into blaming others for one's own behavior

10. flight into self with no surrender to spiritual values

11. flight into following the false prophets of quick cure

12. flight away from the *Journey*

Chapter VI

The Essentials of Affirmation

Beloved, let us love one another; for love is of God, and he who loves is born of God and knows God. He who does not love does not know God; for God is love.

—1 John 4:7

The essentials of affirmation are trust, approval, recognition, appreciation, reconciliation, reverence, and contemplation.

Jesus responded to the adulterous woman with the affirming words "Neither do I condemn you." He saw her guilt and fear, and his response affirmed her inner power to accept herself as she was, to accept her own responsibility, her own sinfulness, and her own need for reconciliation. To affirm is to say yes to whom the person is and in so doing we recognize and revere each person's capacity for growth and healing. The greatest act of trust we can give another is to facilitate and encourage spiritual and emotional growth.

Trust

When I taught high school in New York City I gained the best results from my students by trusting them in my words and actions. To affirm another person is to trust the other's ability to cocreate. Patience and often humility are required of the affirmer to trust the other person's potential to develop.

People often have erroneous notions of trust. It cannot be legislated or even assumed. Trust is a gift which we give gradually to another person. Some persons feel that because they are members of a religious community, family, or club, they must be completely trustful. We should not confuse trust with loyalty, however. Trust goes much deeper and penetrates the very core of the personality. Trust ultimately means vulnerability, and we are often afraid to trust because we do not want people to turn their backs on us. Openness is necessary for trust, which means freedom in relationship, whether these relationships be with friends, associates, or with our significant other. Trust invites us to share our real self rather than an ideal self or the person we think we should be.

Trust is a process which we learn from infancy. It constantly grows and shrinks; it needs consistent nurturing.

In my book *Who Controls Me?* I developed the theme of trust in relationship to identity and the individual.[1] I pointed out that trust is essential to personal identity, to confidence in developing relationships, and to the feeling that one is affirmed. As Erik Erikson points out, trust develops from the child's early relationship with its parents,

---

1. Thomas A. Kane, *Who Controls Me?* (Hicksville, NY: Exposition Press, 1974).

particularly its mother. A survey of some twenty young men in a Boston prison revealed that the one thing they had in common was a failure of parental relationships. In some cases, there was a basic lack of trust; in others, the home was broken up by divorce or the death of a parent and subsequent arrival of a stepparent. If individuals are not trusted and accepted, they will not trust and accept themselves. They will then accept uncritically the behavior of their peer groups and will have no confidence in their own ability to evaluate it.

Our Lord's sense of trust gives us a keen insight into human relationships. Christ's trust in his own judgment was complete. He had received everything from his Father and he would give it all to others. He had no uncertainty, no equivocation. Christ knew whom he wanted as his intimate friends and as his followers, and after the original choice there was no doubt, no experimentation, no withdrawal. His is a model of trust in affirming relationships in which continuity, reliability, and predictability are present.

Even Christ's closest followers, the apostles, found his trust in them difficult because it was so constant in the face of their apparent and explicit weakness, limitations, and sinfulness. We share in the trust Jesus has for all who take to themselves the name of Christ and call themselves Christian. His trust is consistent:

> *I am the good shepherd.*
> *I know my own and my own know me*
> *just as the Father knows me*
> *and I know the Father;*
> *and I lay down my life for my sheep.*
>
> —John 10:14-16

Approval

Approval is derived from the Latin word *probus*, meaning good. To say and feel "it is good that you exist" is an act of approval. This approval is an act of the will which testifies to being in agreement, assenting, consenting, applauding, praising, and affirming the other person. Though all the words in this series differ in intensity, they are all the same in that they are expressions of the free will of a person and mean:

"It is good that you exist."
"I want you to be."

Remember, affirmation is concerned primarily with being. To have sincere good will toward another person is no small thing. Yet, good will is not in itself sufficient to constitute what we mean by approval in the process of affirmation. Thomas Aquinas calls the missing element *unio affectus*. This means that besides wishing another well, we are *moved* toward the person simply because that individual is good. This is approval.

I am reminded of the two versions of the story about the little boy with the fat worm. A five-year-old boy runs to his mother holding a big, fat worm in his hand and says, "Mommy, look what a big, fat worm I've got." She says, "Wonderful, you can go fishing with daddy tomorrow. Now you must wash your hands and prepare for supper." In the other version, the mother replies, "Your hands are dirty. You are filthy. Go away and clean yourself immediately." In the first version the mother approved the young boy; in the latter she lost a valuable opportunity to promote her son's growth.

Recognition

Unfortunately, it seems easier for human beings to point out the negative qualities than to recognize the positive ones in each other. Recognition is important in the process of affirmation, because we openly and honestly acknowledge the good in another person. When we recognize another, we gift them with a reflection of their own intrinsic goodness. We convey the thought and feeling that the person is not only needed but wanted.

The slightest sign of recognition from another at least affirms one's presence in the world. William James once wrote, "No more fiendish punishment could be devised, even were such a thing physically possible, than that one should be turned loose in society and remain absolutely unnoticed by all the members thereof." By reacting indifferently, lukewarmly, or impersonally, one fails to give the recognition so essential in the affirmation process.

Ways of recognition differ, but all are important when we affirm. Recognition can be *visual* (for example, a responsive smile), *tactile* (an embrace), *auditory* (an expression of praise), or *spiritual* (shared prayer). All forms of recognition encourage our brothers and sisters to recognize their own goodness and help them to gently live this life with a degree of happiness.

We must help others to see how certain cultural forces can reduce them to seeking recognition of their needs in ways that are deceptive. Recognition will not be affirming if it comes from having the "right" kinds of possessions: car, home, clothes, liquor, deodorant. The public relations world of advertising knows how vulnerable consumers are, and at times their merchandise, promising to bring recognition, only brings slavery to that particular product. Advertising, as well as certain accepted ideologies, is a cultural demon that needs to be exorcised.

Appreciation

A sense of personal significance is often made an inner reality by the appreciation we receive from others. Appreciation is essential to the growth of affirmation. The appreciation we receive from our parents establishes within us a personal meaning which we retain in their absence. Appreciation in the same sense of personal significance exists in the form of the ability to feel good, lovable, and worthy. This is not merely the acceptance we receive from our parents but the quality of their appreciation of us. They affirm our progressive realization of our own potential to be the persons we want and choose to be.

It is the Christian's task to tell the world that God appreciates it. He loves his creation; he appreciates the world in us and through us and wants to affirm through us. God's appreciation is evident in the Christian church, where all persons can find compassion and assurance of the truth that "despite everything, being is good." In an age in which the face of God is obscured, it is important that we destroy the contempt in our hearts, so that the whole sympathy with being which slumbers within us can break forth, the total affirmation of others, and thus our lives become a "proof of God" for them. To reveal to others that they have been chosen, loved, and named by God; that they are free, responsible cocreators—this is to give appreciation, this is to give life!

Reconciliation

Another essential of affirmation is reconciliation. Reconciliation is not only restoring harmony with someone else. It is making peace within ourselves in that dimension of our lives where we could find no peace. It is seldom an instant catharsis or quick relief from pain, nor is it merely learning to live with that which we know we can never change. Rather, reconciliation is a gentle growth into unity, into feeling that things are coming together in life.

Father Louis Evely points to a beautiful truth about reconciliation. He states that as we enter the confessional or penance room we say, "Bless me, Father, for I have sinned," because I have received this first great grace of realizing that I have sinned. We do not say, "Punish me, Father, tell me off because I have sinned." Rather, we ask, "Father, say a good word to me, encourage me, congratulate me, because God has touched me."[2]

Reconciliation is the manner in which we become reunited with our universe, with others, with ourselves, and with God. Notice that when we seek reconciliation we are not seeking an excuse for our behavior; rather, we are facing our behavior and seeking forgiveness to find the way to unity and peace. Within the process of reconciliation we discover new strength of character and encouragement in the affirming way of life.

Reverence

The theme of this book is that all of God's creation is worthy of reverence, not because of accomplishments on

---

2. Louis Evely, *We Dare to Say Our Father* (New York: Herder and Herder, 1965), p. 100.

the part of the created, but simply because of God's call into existence. When we have experienced the sacredness of being, we place ourselves in the service of life. But this can happen only if we revere life, honor it, affirm it, and assist it to become more beautiful and more alive. We find happiness in life and in the joy of others. Reverence is an essential of affirmation because it motivates us to help others so that they can find their way in life, so that they can free themselves from all that blocks their path to happiness.

We reverence the being of others simply by affirming them, without any other motive. Through us the world experiences that it is alive, beautiful, and worthy of affirmation. Existence becomes happy only if we experience it as happiness, and only in such a way that it notices we are made happy by it. Reverence is making known and feeling the "happy are you" by experiencing others' existence as happiness. Our quiet receptivity and active caring create more light in our world. By affirming the whole of existence, we help to make our world firm and strong.

We reverence others and approve of them by our gentle affirmation that they have within themselves aspects of personality that are good, beautiful, and lovable, something that lies within them as a promise yet to be developed. If we practice affirmation, we cultivate reverence and we become a more whole person.

By revering another person we become ourselves, truly our original selves, but in order to revere another person we must first revere ourselves. However, we can authentically revere our own selves only while revering something within us that absolutely transcends that self: namely, God.

Christ is the man in whom God totally revered humanity. In Christ, God said yes to our whole human nature, with all its pettiness, weakness, and limitations, but at the same time, with all its hope and openness to the absolute. Ladislaus Boros in his beautiful essay "Reverence" reminds us:

> And yet the man who reveres others has already reached the goal. Whenever he sees the absolute in another and lovingly acknowledges it, this absolute streams back to him and man is borne into the incarnate God. This life is a life in God, and yet precisely because of that a life in the world. He is, to the depths of his being, turned towards God. Precisely through this such a man can pour power and life into the world. They [sic] can also be quite simple, even childlike; these men who are truly possessed by Christ are of a strangely enlivening, healing and sanctifying spirit. They are not miracles, but something miraculous appears in them. They live in a state for which early theology had a strange word: *"fruitio Dei,"* "the enjoyment of God." They live in him, perhaps without knowing it, without even thinking about it. In their reverence for God these men have found themselves and their brother.[3]

Contemplation

Reverence of things, others, and self leads to giving of oneself; contemplation originates in a person's giving of self and leads ultimately to human fulfillment. In chapter four I mentioned that affirmation is relationship with God in that we allow the openness and presence of God to affirm us. Contemplation is direct encounter with the Absolute. Whether we do it consciously or unconsciously, all

---

3. Ladislaus Boros, *Meeting God In Man* (Norwich, U. K.: Fletcher and Son, 1967), p. 42.

persons are capable of contemplation because it is an essential of affirmation which is characteristic of human existence.

We may think contemplation is only for monks. This is not true. All Christians are called in varying degrees to contemplative presence with the Lord. In contemplation, God's spirit is free to communicate to us directly without words or images. Like Lazarus, we are always coming out of the darkness of death into the light of Christ's presence. Contemplation allows Christians a new freedom to take their lives into their own hands or to take responsibility for behavior that would be most pleasing to God. As we come to know and feel "God is love" (1 John 4:8), we arrive at a greater appreciation of ourselves and a healthy love of self. My colleague, Vincent M. Bilotta III, captures this truth very well when he writes:

As I experience God as the source of my life, a longing wells up within me, a longing to grow older together with the living fountain of my life.

Upon entering into myself, I find God. By coming to discover my original self, I come to God. As I befriend the silent darkness within me, I become more open to the hidden and mysterious dimension of myself. There, as I rest in the darkness, I uncover myself as gift from God. I need to take up that gift and walk gently and compassionately with the sacredness that I am. I need to affirm the fragile gift that I am. My response to myself as gift calls for a faithful actualizing and unfolding of my personhood as gift. I need to care for the precious gift that I am, preserve it, and hallow the ground from which it springs.

As I embrace the process of being more awakened to my uniqueness, I am affirming the truth that I am and giving honor and glory to God. Responding to the person I am means then that I freely choose to work with God in the creation of my original self. I need to allow myself to become all that I can be.[4]

---

4. Vincent M. Bilotta III, "Originality, Ordinary Intimacy and the Spiritual Life: Welcome! Make Yourself at Home," *Studies In Formative Spirituality Journal* 1 (February 1980): 83.

I have spoken of moving from loneliness to solitude. A state of being alone, of inwardly directed consciousness, solitude is not necessarily physical isolation. In solitude a person claims value for one's self as a free being. The value found in turning inward is the value of self-determination and responsibility. We find self-worth in solitude, in the core of our freedom. Solitude is necessary for spiritual and professional growth; solitude gives us the ability to face ourselves, others, and God.

—Sister Anna Polcino

Chapter VII

The Conditions for Facilitating Affirmation

*The great thing in this world
is not so much where we are,
but in what direction
we are moving.*

—Oliver Wendell Holmes

In the preceding two chapters, I discussed the various obstacles to affirmation and the essentials for living the affirming life. In this chapter, I want to consider some of the facilitating conditions that enable a person to live with a deeper sense of affirmation in daily life. The following diagram is the basis for the first section of this chapter:

TIME

      presence   to be alone
      listening   to be with friends

SPACE   to be with fellow workers
      privacy   to be with God

121

Time

I have frequently mentioned in previous chapters that excessive activity or workaholism is one of the most serious obstacles to living a life of affirmation. "To kill time," a cliche I very much dislike, is heard often on the lips of people who are compulsive doers. Remember, affirmation is concerned primarily with being, secondarily with doing. Compulsive workers follow a relentless schedule and frequently just do not have enough time in a twenty-four-hour day. Such persons need to stop and reflect on the meaning and value of time. They need to *take* time, no matter how busy they are. In order to know themselves, to find some sort of orientation in life, they may have to ignore the schedule, to do as they like for a while, to do nothing but look and listen. Persons who start to take life seriously and graciously realize that on this journey toward happiness "something must give." This something more often than not has to do with how people manage their time. Those gospel people who journeyed to Christ were persons who started to realize the value and importance of time. In embracing a respectful awareness of time, we come closer to being our real selves.

Presence

We know how difficult it is to communicate with persons who are physically present but mentally absent. Such persons can also be unaware of their own presence. By not taking the time to be present to themselves, they often exist taking this life for granted. Other people are kept at a comfortable distance, and there is little room in such a life for the mystery of caring for others.

We have all met people who radiate an inner presence. We feel as though they know us well and though we spend only a few moments with them, their presence leaves us with a special feeling of our own importance and dignity.

Listening

"You hear me but you do not listen" is heard all too frequently between married couples and friends. Yet, if the marriage or friendship is to flourish, it is essential that we develop an awareness that reverencing time and presence facilitates our ability to listen to others and ourselves. In listening to self and others, we come closer to our real world of mystery, vulnerability, and the goodness of life. The more we develop the art of listening, the more we grow in our ability to gently affirm others. We become less controlling and freer in allowing others to share in our world of weakness as well as strength. We give up the illusion that we can "make it" alone in this life and we allow others to care for us as unique human beings. The listening attitude, in a sense, allows me to see that in reality I do not really possess myself or others. We are nobody's property. A listening attitude allows growth and a certain comfortableness with happiness and joy as well as with sorrow and suffering. Herein, we discover the respectful presence of God in ourselves and others.

Space

As a priest, I have the privilege to be welcomed into the homes of open and hospitable people. A home is a place of love, and as Paul writes, *"amor edificat"* ("love builds") (1 Cor. 8:1): love builds a place which is called home. The home is that place, that space where we can be ourselves and relax and be present to family or friends. Space is very important if home is truly to be a place of love.

Each room speaks of the use of space and how it relates to building a home. The living room, the dining room, the bedroom, the kitchen, the bathroom, all speak to the importance of space for individual growth. Everyone, no matter what vocation in life, needs to develop a respectful attitude toward space.

Throughout religious tradition there has always been "sacred" space for the worship of the Creator. Temple, church, or mosque, all point to humanity's inner need to foster respectful use of space.

In our technological age, space becomes even more important. We are inhabitants of earth. Overcrowded city living or isolated country living, neither of which foster connection with other families or individuals, can be equally devastating to a life that affirms the goodness of persons. When we affirm our world, we become acutely aware of the need to plan space, to appropriate space, to protect space.

Unfortunately for many of my fellow priests and religious, the social and economic situation of the religious life often does not value the sanctity of space. We protect and plan sacred space for worship, but we often have very little genuine living space in which to relax and be ourselves. The more priests and religious slow down from their apostolic workaholism, the more they take a look at the space in their lives. Our effectiveness will be impaired if we deny ourselves a home away from our work. We need space, as do other human beings, for privacy and an opportunity to be away from our work. This does not and should not mean that we are less available to the needs of the people we serve.

Father Paul Keyes, who has greatly influenced my thoughts about space, comments on the need for space in rectory living:

> A rectory should have work space, living together space, and private space. In many rectories these three separate spaces get mixed together. With regard to work space, I think priests have to be more aware of what a cold and lifeless room means, not only to themselves, but to the many people who visit this room. In many rectories one can find cramped little rooms in which Father is expected to carry on his "business" with parishioners. Such rooms are usually filled with a big desk that takes up most of the space. Father is expected to sit behind the desk and fill out forms, whereas parishioners are left to sit on old rickety chairs that should have been sold as antiques many years ago. Some "modern" priests have felt that folding steel chairs are the best way to save space in cramped offices. The problem with meeting people in rooms that are merely functionally oriented is that usually people cannot feel at home. I cannot ever imagine Christ sitting behind a desk and meeting people in some of the rooms that we call offices. No human being in his right mind can ever feel at home in such a milieu. The magnificence of Christ's care was that people were able to feel at home in his presence. If feeling at home was the mystery of Christ's caring presence, I have to think seriously about how I offer rectory space as a sign of hospitable care.[1]

Time and Space "To Be"

A Jesuit priest from India came to study at the House of

---

1. Paul T. Keyes, *Pastoral Presence and the Diocesan Priest* (Whitinsville, MA: Affirmation Books, 1978), p. 83.

Affirmation in Whitinsville, Massachusetts. He wrote the following in a term paper he gave to me:

> From around the age of eight, almost every day at Mass when the priest was raising the consecrated Host at the elevation, I was praying: "Lord, make me a priest." Then when I joined the Society of Jesus, and began to read the lives of the saints during my novitiate, I began to add to my above petition, "Lord, make me a saint." But now, in my early forties, I have begun to pray, "Lord, make me a man." Am I regressing or progressing?

Like so many of my students, this good priest was growing out of the illusion that God only cares for perfect people and that to be a good priest he must become a perfect saint. He was learning anew that Christ entered the world because God loved sinners. Jesus Christ is the man of scriptures who walked and ate with sinners. His closest friends, the apostles, were ordinary people with shortcomings and imperfections. Peter, the first pope, the rock upon which Jesus built his Church, crumbled to pieces in his denial of the master. Finally, Peter, like all followers of Christ, came to realize that the true rock was Jesus. On the rock of Christ's presence in his life, Peter built the foundation of the early Church.

As we slow down we come to realize that we are persons called in time and space *to be* freely and fully human and that therein is our sanctity. We see that an individual life is a *gift* entrusted to us freely and generously by God himself. When I struggle to live a life of affirmation, I must ultimately let go of trying to control all the variables of existence and surrender in faith to the freeing power of the providential plan. This only happens when I emphasize in my day-to-day life the time and place *to be* alone, *to be* with friends, *to be* with fellow workers, and *to be* with God.

Limits

Limit need not be an oppressive word. A family or community which affirms its own members will promote discussion and understanding of limits while at the same time allowing for emotional growth. Members will feel understood. The group thus encourages flexibility while creating an atmosphere of adequacy and stability. The awareness of the mutual responsibility of the individual toward community and community toward the individual creates a security that serves to absorb the temporary periods of anxiety that any member of the group may sustain. This awareness of the dynamics of family or community life maintains unity during inevitable periods of anger or disagreement.

Anger

The mention of disagreement leads us to another condition for facilitating affirmation. Each family or community must develop the capability of the group as a whole and of each of its members to allow and accept expressions of anger. When we come together in community from different backgrounds, each with our own personality differences, it is inevitable that conflict and anger will arise. We have to give up the idea that there is any such thing as a perfect family, perfect priest, perfect religious, or perfect community.

Obviously, we know anger occurs. The cold shoulder pattern is a common and destructive way of expressing anger. There are more creative ways of expressing and accepting anger, however, that will not destroy individuals or the group as a whole. We must give up the tendency to suffer too much. Encouraging the expression of anger does not mean that the origin of the anger should not be actively explored by the group. Far too often anger is used as a psychological tool to manipulate the group or one another. This sort of testing must be examined for what it really is. One never allows anger to obscure the consequences of action. An illustration of this point can be found in the individual who for the sake of "peace and harmony" avoids all possible areas of conflict, all anger, even to the extent of sacrificing principles which should be asserted. I have that "peace and harmony" cliche in quotes because it does so much damage to real peace and authentic harmony. When we know there is no peace and no harmony, let us deal with reality and not play games.

Anger is not a reason to avoid facing reality. We should not allow any member of the group to use anger for the purpose of playing on the guilt of others or for playing the game of "who takes the blame this time?" When we try to ignore or escape from the inevitable differences of opinion or of interest, we do so at the price of becoming submissive to others and negating our own sense of individuality and dignity. Without the expression of anger and resentment, it is impossible for people to know each other and to meet each other's important and realistic needs. Too often in a family or community where feelings are not expressed there exist unresolved and unhealthy dependency struggles, rather than a mutual acceptance of realistic and shared needs.

I think I speak to the experience of many when I say that for too long within a family or community we have expected ourselves not to be angry. It is a healthy sign when we can get angry and express that anger within a group without fear of rejection.

The group, too, must deal with anger responsibly and not allow us or any other member of the group to manipulate everyone with our anger. In the inevitable situations of discord within the family or community, we must maturely assesss the expression of anger. How many of us would be helped in our growth and development if someone would say, "Really, you overreacted. Your anger is out of proportion to the situation!" Such a response is a real help. It facilitates healing and does not allow anger to smolder unresolved.

Dependency Needs

Another condition for facilitating affirmation is an atmosphere where there is mutual fulfillment of normal dependency needs. Such an atmosphere allows us to feel relaxed and emotionally secure within the family or community. Thus, we are free to express honest feelings and needs. When the expression of one's feelings and thoughts is accepted (though not necessarily agreed with), each person within the group will become a more effective adult.

Notice that I say normal dependency needs. I do not believe we can be fully mature or can think about mature lifestyles if our dependency needs are not somewhat fulfilled. We must feel free to say to the community members, "I need you." Too often adults have said, "I need no one." Living in isolation and speaking frequently of community, many persons have lived and still live without knowing the fulfillment of meaningful communication. There must be mutual identification, mutual awareness of our dependence on each other as fellow human beings.

If family or community members have an accurate awareness of the strengths and weaknesses of each other, then expectations will be based on supportive and realistic appraisals of who each person is. There will be no magical ideas of perfect success and no fears of total failure. Adaptation to any situation is always a relative matter; we all succeed and we all fail to a certain degree. It is the achievement of more successes than failures which results in good mental health.

The fulfillment of our normal dependency needs is, in part, why we are a family or community. Before we can be fully and maturely independent we must have experienced dependence in a healthy way. I do not mean that we must infantilize ourselves, but that in order to be a mature adult I need a group, a community, a family, upon which I can depend. I need that kind of support and acceptance. I need the support group to reflect my own goodness back to me and take delight in it. The group that denies and does not affirm the goodness of its members is on a path of inevitable self-destruction.

Each person has good days and bad days. Most group members are able to be effective adults most of the time. From time to time members will have feelings of doubt and inadequacy about themselves and their group. Growth comes when the community allows them to be intimately dependent. Then such persons can express doubts, feelings of uncertainty and inadequacy, and significant others in the group can help them to explore the causes and meanings of such internalized conflicts. In this way the community provides its members with an opportunity for achieving personality growth and healing.

Self-Sufficiency

Healthy coping in family or community will necessarily mean that each group member has attained a certain level of self-sufficiency. We have already touched upon this matter in previous paragraphs. The group can help each person to act with self-sufficiency by creating an atmosphere where rivalry is inappropriate and by not allowing rivalry to be part of the unspoken structure.

Self-sufficiency allows for multiple approaches to the same issue; yet it need not lead to polarization if the group members realize that the common good is of the essence to their communal endeavor. Self-sufficiency can bring about creative insight, spontaneous joy, and pride in the community of which they are members. Decision making and accountability become opportunities for a comfortable belongingness and not oppressive burdens. Self-sufficiency in a family or community can be a disheartening experience or it can be a fascinating exercise in communal communication.

Competition

Competition is an element that makes communal living very frustrating. Some family or community behavior fosters the rivalry created between two people in order to enhance the relationship of one of them with a third party, usually an authority figure. This kind of rivalry leads to childish dependence and not to the kind of normal, effective reliance on each other that enhances adult life.

When one feels self-sufficient and has resolved childish dependency needs, there is no need to idealize persons in authority and there is no need to be suspicious of normal friendship. True self-sufficiency leans toward normal dependence upon the group. Self-sufficiency should not be confused with a feeling of omnipotence; people with such feelings are not really self-sufficient, but have established fears and distance so as to maintain their own masks of noninvolvement in communal goals, dreams, and apostolates. Knowing I am part of a community but still self-sufficient does not mean that I spread myself so thin that I can control all variables or assume that I have more power than I really have. I am not always in competition. Self-sufficiency puts competition in the proper perspective and allows me to relate to the other community members in the way that is most meaningful and compelling.

Loneliness

The last condition for facilitating affirmation in a family or community which we will briefly reflect upon is loneliness.

The nonaffirmed person displays a lifestyle marked by doing, workaholism, and escapism, always in an effort to run away from loneliness. The nonaffirmed person looks to work, power, possessions, pleasing people, and "killing time" as ways of evading the reality of loneliness.

Several years ago Clark Moustakas wrote a book entitled *Loneliness* in which he distinguished two types of loneliness: loneliness anxiety and existential loneliness. Nonaffirmed persons suffer from loneliness anxiety, which results from the breach between what a person is and what he or she pretends to be. Lonely persons so dread their loneliness that they engage in a continuous attempt to escape it. Their efforts are futile, however. No crowd, no title, no new "authentic psychological theory" can take away the reality that each of us is a solitary individual, that each of us is uniquely alone in this world. Existential loneliness is our awareness of ourselves as solitary persons. Moustakas urges that we "let be" our loneliness. Our separateness offers us the opportunity to grow in awareness of creative loneliness, through the experience of which we learn about our relatedness to others and to all of creation.[2]

The affirmed person does not run away from loneliness but experiences it as an existential reality. Affirmed persons share their loneliness and in sharing it come to a new knowledge and feeling of self. Moustakas speaks of this experience when he writes:

> We must care for our own loneliness and suffering and the loneliness and suffering of others, for within pain and isolation and loneliness one can find courage and hope and what is brave and lovely and true in life. Seeing loneliness is a way to self-identity and to love, and faith in the wonder of living.
>
> . . . Loneliness leaves its traces in man but these are marks of pathos, of weathering, which enhance dignity and maturity and beauty, and which open new possibilities for tenderness and love. . . . Loneliness is as much a reality of life as night and rain and thunder and it can be lived creatively. So I say let there be loneliness, for where there is loneliness, there is also sensitivity, there is awareness and recognition of promise.[3]

---

2. Clark Moustakas, *Loneliness and Love* (Englewood Cliffs, NJ: Prentice Hall, 1972), p. 103.
3. Ibid.

We can creatively develop a sense of unlonely aloneness. We can enjoy spending time by ourselves doing things we enjoy. We must have time alone to commune with God, to know the nature of relationship with others, and to understand commitment to the community and to ourselves. We gain a coherent and sustaining way of life not only from our community but also from the sense of faith that emerges clearly from our experience of loneliness and from our need for increased communication and sharing.

Try to remember when life was so tender
That no one wept except the willow.
Try to remember when life was so tender
That dreams were kept beside the pillow.

—''The Fantasticks''

Chapter VIII

The Fruits of Affirmation

Nothing is so strong
as gentleness;
Nothing is so gentle
as real strength.

—Francis de Sales

I doubt that there is today any one person who more typifies the fruits of affirmation—assertiveness and gentleness—than our present Holy Father, John Paul II. Deliberate in speech, unshakable in principle and yet inviting in presence, he imparts kindness in his approach to varied cultures around the world.

Often people associate affirmation with "people pleasing" behavior. Trying to be the "nice guy," the "soft-spoken lady," the person who attempts to suit everyone, leaves one with little sense of self-worth, integrity, or dignity. Let us again turn to some written statements from former clients:

> I don't want to be a women's libber. I just won't ask for what are my perfect rights. In a shopping line, I let people push ahead or I become afraid of the salesperson and buy things I never wanted or needed. When really provoked, I speak up in a very destructive and angry way and nothing is accomplished.
>
> *—Housewife*

> One thing in life I believe I must accomplish is to have everyone I come in contact with like me. Yet, over the years, I find that increasingly difficult. No matter how hard I try, it seems I run into people or situations where I don't get approval. I feel that I don't dare give my own opinions for fear of being put down.
>
> *—Priest*

> I am a student and need to study a great deal if I am going to pass my exams. However, I live in a dormitory and share a room with another person. This person is an excellent student and doesn't need to study as much as I do. She is often noisy and invites her friends into the room while I am trying to study. I sit at my desk, burning with anger inside me. I just won't tell people when they inconvenience me or take advantage of my inability to stand up for what I know is correct.
>
> *—Female College Student*

> Suffering is part of the Christian life. My mother is in her sixties, is in good health, but constantly makes me feel guilty for not giving her more of my time. I am a religious sister and with all my obligations I have little

free time. I very seldom join other community members for relaxation, because I feel so obligated to mother, and she lives only a short distance away. I offer it up, but inside I know that I am under a lot of internal mental and physical stress.

—*Religious Sister*

I am on a diet. It seems that if I watch what I eat, then my health is better because of the weight control. However, I have to eat out a lot and socialize frequently. My friends are always pressing me to try their "famous cheese cake" or some other food that I don't need and really do not want. But, I just can't say no! My mother brings over a big pan of lasagna as a peace offering. (The Lord knows that I've appreciated her lasagna for the last seventeen years.) I don't want to be fat, but I am too sensitive to assert myself.

—*Male Business Executive*

My apartment leaves much to be desired. I am paying top rent. The place is in need of repair and in the winter there is little heat. I snub the landlord every time I see him, because he has ignored my requests. I get so angry at him. Yet, my next-door neighbor seems to get what she needs repaired. I never seem to accomplish much in arguments, because I come across in such an angry and hostile fashion.

—*Female Office Worker*

Just about every time I go to a party, a drink of liquor is offered. I enjoy one drink. But in order not to offend anyone, I usually take more than I want or can handle. When I get home I am usually a little sick. I really don't enjoy drinking. I feel so bad and remorseful that I always give in and do things I do not want to do.

—*Male University Student*

I am often asked for my opinion by my superior, but I never really give it. I always tell people, especially authority figures, just what I think they want to hear. The result of this is that I hate myself for ending up with things other than the way I want them, or with too much work. My nonassertive behavior seems to reinforce my low opinion of myself.

—Religious Brother

Assertion or Aggression

If we are aggressive, we tend to attack people or ideas. When we are assertive, we speak up for our own rights without infringing on the rights of others, and, in the process, improve our own self-image. I assert my ideas or feelings directly and honestly while allowing the other person to do the same. Assertiveness can teach us to look at ourselves and our behavior honestly and to express other wants openly without hidden or passive-aggressive agenda.

Aggressive people play many roles but ultimately these roles are destructive to personality growth. Such persons usually put themselves first, walk over others, bully them, are not willing to compromise, and talk behind people's backs. Their arrogance is often frightening. Aggressive people can also hide behind a shy but false facade; their shyness is just another opportunity to grumble and complain or to play the poor me or martyr role.

Assertive behavior is as different from aggressive behavior as fat is from thin.

Aggression attacks	Assertion respects
Aggression creates hostility	Assertion smooths the way
Aggression tramples	Assertion joins forces
Aggression irritates	Assertion soothes
Aggression antagonizes	Assertion gains respect
Aggression produces guilt	Assertion develops self-respect

Selfishness or Humility

The "assertion" that pop psychology stresses is many times nothing more than old-fashioned selfishness or rudeness. Militant in tone and aggressive in manner, it often is merely an effective tool with which to put people down. Selfish and rude persons want things their own way and will allow little negotiation, compromise, or tolerance. Aggressive behavior puts people at a distance and fosters isolation. Growth in affirmation means growing out of nonassertive or aggressive behavior into an assertive posture. Continued nonassertion tends to leave the individual depressed and feeling like everyone's doormat. I often tell my clients that the affirmed person will have enemies. Not that we want enemies, but if we stand firm and do not allow others to violate us, we run the risk of being disliked.

Christian concern for one's neighbor is not obsolete.

What I am speaking about is a respectful approach to persons, a way of integrity and prudence that comes from a true understanding of humility. God commands us to love our neighbor as ourselves. If we and others have been created in the image of God as Genesis insists, we have no right to despise God's handiwork. Too often nonassertive behavior has been identified with humility, and assertion has been confused with the sin of pride. In this connection, it is refreshing to recall that Saint Thomas Aquinas's definition of humility is "the reasonable pursuit of one's own excellence."[1] We could hardly find a more psychologically healthy statement. We have a God-given excellence and we are called to develop it in accordance with reason. Pride, then, would be the unreasonable pursuit of our own excellence. Nonassertive behavior in regard to our personal integrity and aggressive behavior toward others do violence to God's plan.

The Assertive Church

To be assertive as a person leaves us feeling good, even though assertion can be uncomfortable at times. The Church obeys the teachings of the Divine Physician when it brings healing to society by asserting and protecting fundamental truths, regardless of their popularity. The abortion issue is of real concern for many people in the world today. Though unpopular with some sectors of society, the Church must be assertive in protecting family life and the rights of the unborn. This does not mean that Christians should or must become hostile or aggressive toward those

---

1. Thomas Aquinas as quoted by Martin W. Pable, "Christian Personality Development," *The Priest* 33 (March 1977): 12.

who disagree with them. Simply, assertiveness will not allow one's rights, territory, or principles to be violated.

Growth in Assertion

Learning to assert ourselves effectively and meaningfully is a path to affirming others and to opening ourselves to the affirmation of others. Each person's needs and wants are important. Assertiveness education can help us to communicate these needs. There are many good assertiveness training programs available and several good books on the topic as well. One of the earliest and best books on the difference between assertion and aggression, with a guide on how to grow out of nonassertive behavior, is *Your Perfect Right: A Guide to Assertive Behavior* by Robert Alberti and Michael Emmons.[2] In regard to workshops or seminars, remember that these are only educational opportunities and not counseling or psychotherapy. Beware of any program that promises magic results or a quick way to assertive behavior. It takes time, risk, and sincerity to venture out of nonassertive or aggressive behavior until we experience satisfaction from attempts to grow in affirmation. Be gentle with yourself.

Gentleness

It may seem strange to some that I have called assertion and gentleness the fruits of affirmation. However, when we grow in affirmation of others and receive love from others, we are able to be both strong and gracious. Often, one of the most difficult instructions I can give people is to "be gentle with yourself."

---

2. Robert E. Alberti and Michael L. Emmons, *Your Perfect Right: A Guide to Assertive Behavior* (San Luis Obispo, CA: Impact Publishers, 1970).

Jesus speaks to us when he says, ". . . learn from me, for I am gentle and humble of heart. Your souls will find rest" (Matt. 11:29). When we struggle to live the life of affirmation, we come to know and feel something of this intimate gentleness of Jesus as we see it reflected in our world, our neighbors, and ourselves.

In his book *Spirituality and the Gentle Life*, Father Adrian Van Kaam gives us an original and comprehensive study of gentleness as the facilitating condition and fruit of the Holy Spirit.[3] Van Kaam explains that gentleness does not point to a thing but to a person's attitude. Gentleness is usually sparked by something that is precious but vulnerable. A baby, little children, the victim of a tragedy, a holy person, a newborn puppy, a sick person, or the elderly can evoke gentleness. Strength and power do not elicit gentleness as much as do the fragility and the vulnerability of the precious treasure of life. All that is delicate, innocent, and umblemished can, consequently, invite our gentleness. We experience it in our gentle response to a young child not yet tarnished by the hard ways of the world. We feel gentle in the presence of a beautiful rose, the loneliness of a human face, and the dignity of gracious music. Any person, place, thing, or situation that mirrors the precious fragility of life brings forth the gentle person within us. All that is beautiful can make us gentle for it can be marred so easily.

Gentle With Myself

Father Van Kaam's beautiful book presents the basic question of the affirming life: can I be gentle with myself?

---

3. Adrian Van Kaam, *Spirituality and the Gentle Life* (New Jersey: Dimension Books, 1974), pp. 28-29.

I can be gentle with myself only if I will allow others to affirm me and if I accept my own personal experience of being precious, fragile, and vulnerable. We all know from everyday living that we are not always faithful to our inner call to gentleness.

"Forgive Us"

The first prayer many of us ever learned was the Our Father, and during our lifetime we pray daily: "Forgive us our trespasses, as we forgive those who trespass against us." The number one problem for most people in their search for gentleness is to learn to forgive themselves. The person who does the most trespassing against me is I myself. Many times we feel disappointed with ourselves. We feel that we have not measured up. We refuse to accept our shortcomings and limitations.

The Gift

The first step in being gentle with myself is to affirm the reality that I am a unique gift. I have to learn to admit and accept weakness, for we are fragile earthen vessels of great value. We have to accept our own vulnerability and feet of clay. Only when others affirm me and I open myself to their affirmation will I take delight in the fact that I am a unique but limited person called forth from my very birth to be gentle and congenial. In a true sense, the gentle person is strong enough to be weak. Van Kaam reminds us:

> In living the gentle life style, I may discover something else. It becomes easier for me to pray, to meditate, to stay attuned to God's presence. Gentility stills and quiets the greediness and aggressiveness of the ego. A silenced ego allows me to center myself in my

divine ground. While it is helpful to have a strong ego, it is harmful to center my life in that ego alone. Greediness and arrogance might then absorb all of my life. I would be so busy keeping my ego sublime, sane, and successful that no time would be left for a gentle nursing of my soul in the light of God's gentility.

Any true gentility, human or divine, mellows the ego, not by weakening its strength but by diminishing its arrogance, its false exclusiveness, its pretense of ultimacy. Any diminishment of the ego's arrogance makes me more available to the Divine.

Van Kaam continues:

The asceticism of the gentle life style is already a path to God's presence. Once I live in that presence my gentility may deepen and gain a quality it could never obtain by asceticism alone. It is deepened by a divine gift; it becomes a peace that passes understanding, a peace the world cannot give. Because it is a gift, I must ask God to grant it to me. My very beseeching will remind me that evangelical gentility is His gift, not my doing. This reminder is important. For I may forget my dependence on the Divine during my self-preparation for this that complements and transforms my human gentility. God wants me to do what is humanly possible to grow daily in gentility. My effort shows my good will, my increasing readiness for His gift of gentility, when it comes to me in His own good time.

My human attempt to live the gentle life is my promise of cooperation with the grace of gentility once it touches my life. The human attempt to grow in gentility is necessary, yet it may tempt me to forget that its outcome is only provisional, a shadow of things to come— the real thing being the divine gentleness of soul that is a pure gift of the Holy.[4]

---

4. Ibid.

Contradictions?

There may seem to be some contradiction in encouraging both the growth in affirmation (which means gentleness as well as assertion) and a creative use of anger. Gentleness starts when I accept my brokenness before humanity and God, and this brokenness implies that at times I will be angry. To be fearful of exerting my rights or expressing my anger is a way of *not* being gentle with self.

Anger need not be an emotion that is harmful to human relationships. Biblical writers decried any expression of anger which was directed destructively against another person. Paul recognized that anger is not pathological per se when he said, "Be angry, but do not sin. Do not let the sun go down on your anger" (Eph. 4:26). He was advising us to be gentle with the feelings of anger and to express these feelings quickly, directly, and appropriately without bearing a grudge. In later writings, Paul instructed us on the proper objects of anger when he told us to hate such things as theft, murder, coveting, envy, slander, and pride.

We can be angry with evil behavior but not with the person who commits the evil deed. Paul's teaching in paraphrase is: be angry at things about people, but not with people, even though people do things to incite anger. Think about some person whom you do not like. Is it really the person you do not like or perhaps just some of that individual's behavior?

In the next chapter, we will reflect on the characteristics of an affirmed person and learn how one woman and one man were able to integrate assertion and gentleness within an affirming lifestyle.

to be
affirmed
is having
a known
and inner
awareness
of your own felt
goodness

T. A. Kane

Chapter IX

The Characteristics of an Affirmed Person

Happiness cannot come from without.
It must come from within.
It is not what we see and touch
or that which others do for us
which makes us happy;
it is that which we think and feel and do,
first for the other fellow
and then for ourselves.

—Helen Keller

In a sense, this entire book is about the characteristics of affirmation. However, in this chapter I wish to reflect briefly on three very significant characteristics that are most observable in an affirmed person; namely, an attitude of leisure, an attitude of play, and an attitude of celebration. As our examples of affirmed persons we will look to the remarkable young woman of Lisieux, Saint Therese, and to the man whose thirty days as pope left the world

149

some moments of joy that will be remembered for ages, Pope John Paul I.

Leisure

Persons in modern society are very much defined in terms of what they *do*. People feel compelled to fill their daily schedules with activity. At this time in history, when there is so much more time for leisure, people feel guilty when they have free time, and it becomes a burden. Activity is such a way of life for us that only doing and working seem to be meaningful and worthwhile. We rush around as though being busy were a proof of our importance and worth. Excessive activity and workaholism prevent a reflective life of affirmation.

Leisure is an attitude that balances contemporary life. A life of affirmation with time and space for leisure emphasizes being, not doing. Free time is more available to many people today, and they wonder what to do with it. My advice is simply to enjoy it, stay with it. But, we must be careful to note that free time is only potentially leisure. More than any quantity of time, leisure is a quality of life; it is an attitude toward life which presents an opportunity to be.

Josef Pieper, in his remarkable and significant book *Leisure, The Basis of Culture*, defines leisure as "a mental and spiritual attitude—it is not merely the result of external factors, it is not the inevitable result of spare time, a holiday, a week-end, or a vacation. It is, in the first place, an attitude of the mind, a condition of the soul, and as such is utterly contrary to the ideal of the 'worker' in each and every one of the three aspects. . .: work as activity, as toil, as a social function."[1]

Leisure is the opposite of work for work's sake. Neither laziness nor tardiness, leisure offers the opportunity to live the reflective life that leads to the way of affirmation. Leisure implies an attitude of reflection, of nonactivity, of inward calm, of silence, of not being busy and just letting things happen. It is an opportunity to be idle and to open oneself to the whole of creation.

Play

The two most useless things in life are probably prayer and play. In a government or society based solely on utilitarian values, or the work ethic, prayer and play are the first things to be neglected because apparently "they do not serve the work of the state." To develop an attitude of reflective openness to all of creation is to develop a child's sense of wonder and delight in all that is. The attitude of play allows the mind and heart to turn to the essential of life which is contemplation; that is, being present to the truth. Play allows us to shed our workaday seriousness and to give ourselves over to the joy of the Lord's works rather than our own.

Through play we can enjoy risk, mystery, and spontaneity; we do not have to control everything. "Casting our cares on the Lord" helps us to be flexible, gentle, soft, and joyful. Playfulness helps us to mitigate seriousness and to dull the edge of anxious alertness so that we can have those

---

1. Josef Pieper, *Leisure, the Basis of Culture* (New York: The New American Library, 1963), p. 38.

intimate moments in which we intuitively experience the Divine Presence.

Celebration

Celebration is at the center of leisure and play, and it is the basis of worship. Celebration is certainly the scriptural way of life. The Israelites were able to understand their own existence through their experience of God's saving presence and personal affirmation. Their response was to celebrate spontaneously, to rejoice in sharing God's gifts. The psalms consistently invite us to take delight in the Lord, to glorify him and to thank him. We Christians are essentially called to accept God's love as expressed in all of creation, in all the events of daily life, and in the person of Jesus. Every discovery we make of our relationship to God, to self, to others, and to things, is a reason for celebration. Mature Christian life is essentially affirmation of the happiness of creation and is a continual thanksgiving for sharing in the life of God.

John Paul I

Albino Luciani, John Paul I, was a wonderful example of the affirmed person. *Time* magazine referred to him as "a light that left us amazed." One month as pope was enough for him to conquer the hearts and ennoble the spirit of our world. In that short time he carried out an amazing revolution in the history of humanity. An unknown and unlikely candidate for the papacy, his election allowed the world to stop and reflect on the beauty and attractiveness of affirmation. Like Jesus, his simple and captivating words, personal serenity and infectious smile, warm human manner, and unique spiritual depth gave the world a moment of freshness and joy.

This man, who for only thirty days walked in the shoes of Peter, was radiantly happy in proclaiming the Good News and affirming the goodness of God's creation. He, as every human person could see, found joy in love, joy in being, joy in knowledge, joy in truth, and, above all, joy in the mission and message of the Church of which he was supreme pastor. Pope John Paul I witnessed to an unbelieving world the freeing value of a strong and uncluttered faith in the Lord and his Church.

Saint Therese

John Paul I wrote beautifully and intimately about his fondness for Saint Therese of Lisieux. He spoke of her as though he knew her personally when he wrote:

> To God's compassionate love you had offered yourself as victim. All this did not prevent you from enjoying beautiful and good things: before your final illness, you painted joyously, wrote poems and little sacred plays, interpreting roles in some of them with the taste of a sensitive actress. In your last illness, during a moment of remission, you asked for some chocolate pastries. You were not afraid of your own imperfections, nor even of having sometimes dozed off in weariness during meditation.
>
> Loving your neighbor, you drove yourself to render little services, useful but unobserved, and to prefer, when possible, the people who irked you and had least in common with you. Behind their not very likable faces, you sought the lovable face of Christ. And this effort, this seeking, was not noticed. "Mystical as she is in chapel and at work," the mother superior wrote of you,

"she is equally comical and full of fun during recreation, when she makes us split our sides laughing."[2]

Therese spent the last nine years of her life at the Lisieux Carmel. Her sisters recognized her as a good nun, nothing more. She was conscientious and capable. She worked in the chapel, cleaned the dining room, painted pictures, composed pious playlets for the sisters, wrote poems, and loved the intense community prayer life of the cloister. Superiors appointed her to instruct the novices of the community. Externally there was nothing remarkable about this Carmelite nun.

But Therese Martin was caught up in an exchange of love with Christ so dynamic and profound that her whole being was affirmed. She had every right to say as Paul did: "I live, now not I, but Christ lives in me" (Gal. 2:20). We would never know about this hidden life if it were not for the fact that her sister Pauline, who had become prioress of the Lisieux Carmel, ordered Therese to write her autobiography. The book, entitled *The Story of a Soul*, was published in 1898, one year after Therese's death. The trickle of two thousand copies that constituted the first printing has since swelled to millions, and it has been translated into over thirty languages. The autobiography has captivated people of every state and condition of life; it has universal appeal. It is an astounding document that somehow touches the heart of the contemporary person.

The book reveals Therese Martin. As a girl and a young woman she was charmingly candid, endowed with a sense of humor, keenly responsive to people and nature, and

---

2. Albino Luciani (John Paul I), *Illustrissimi*, (Boston, MA: Little, Brown and Company, 1978), p. 146.

sensitive. In many ways Therese was unconventional. She did not care for spiritual treatises; she abhorred retreats. She loved the Blessed Mother but could not stand saying the rosary. In an age when frequent communion was discouraged, she remarked that Christ did not come to Eucharist to remain in a golden ciborium.

Though all these things are interesting, they do not explain her appeal. Why does she attract contemporary persons? Why is it that many serious thinkers point to her as a "beacon of light" in the darkness of our times? Affirmation—that is the word. That is what Therese Martin was all about. From her earliest days she was fascinated by affirmation and determined to plumb its depths regardless of personal cost. She was a woman driven by a strong desire to unlock nothing else but the mystery of life itself. "How," she cried out, "can a soul as imperfect as mine aspire to the possession of love?" The key to Therese Martin's personality was assertiveness and gentleness. Although imperfect, she was determined to reach out and affirm and be receptive to the affirmation of others and God.

She symbolized herself as a little flower. The symbol was gracious. Her purpose in using it was to explain that, like a tiny wild flower in the forest, she survived and indeed flourished through all the seasons of the year, through the warmth of spring and summer as well as the winds and snows of fall and winter.

Therese developed her doctrine of abandonment and love at a time when much of Christianity stressed the fear of God. She bravely flew in the face of religious convention because she could not accept that God would ever reject his children.

Like Christ, she recognized that souls were to be won through the mystery of suffering, and it was to this she dedicated her life. She wanted to affirm people the way Christ affirmed them, but she knew this was impossible. Yet this was the commandment that God had given. So, the only way for her to fulfill the commandment was to let Jesus affirm her and love through her. Thus, she had to abandon herself to him. She came before him with all of her faults and failings. She was not put off by them, knowing that he was merciful and would quickly forgive them. Therese was aware of her littleness. "It is impossible for me to grow up, so I must bear with myself such as I am with all my imperfections. But I want to seek out a means of going to heaven by a little way, a way that is very straight, very short and totally new."

Therese died very young of consumption, offering herself as a recipient of God's affirmation. Her life of twenty-four years was without remarkable external events, but it was filled with inner riches, devotion, and affirmation of self, others, creation, and God.

The Nonaffirmed Affirmers

Therese is a good example of someone who had more than her share of inhibitions and fears, which at times made it difficult for her to love others and to receive love. Sometimes writers in the area of affirmation tell us that only fully and totally affirmed persons can affirm others. However, in my experience, we can affirm even in weakness.

Therese of Lisieux and John Paul I can give us the courage to struggle toward growth in the adult world. At times, my clients feel that they have not affirmed anyone despite their efforts. The apparent contradiction is that they have given strength and firmness to others; they have affirmed despite their own pain or personal lack of affirmation. Unfortunately, they have received few emotional dividends because of the lack of maturation in their emotional life. Yet, in the words of Sir James Barrie: "Those who bring sunshine to the lives of others cannot keep it from themselves."

Chapter X

The Ministry of Affirmation:
"Affirm Your Brothers and Sisters"

—Luke 22:32

Throughout this book I have mentioned my ministry of healing at the House of Affirmation. Now, I would like to tell you something of the story of our affirmation family. I have chosen to do so by printing here for the first time a talk I was invited to deliver in Rome in November 1979. This invitation was extended by Father Pedro Arrupe, S.J. and Father Eugene Cuskelly, M.S.C., on behalf of the Union of Superiors General for Men. For me to be the chief expert and deliver the major address at the meeting was a great personal privilege. It was also an honor that our ministry at the House of Affirmation would be so highly respected as for me to be invited to speak to such a distinguished group of Church leaders from around the world. Present as gracious listeners were Cardinal Eduardo Pironio and Archbishop Augustin Mayer of the Sacred Congregation for Religious and Secular Institutes, and several of their staff members.

His Holiness, Pope John Paul II, sent the following message via Cardinal Casaroli:

> Deeply grateful for the expression of devotedness sent also in the name of the Superiors General meeting to study the theme "Confirma Fratres Tuos," the sovereign pontiff offers wishes for fruitful conclusions in view of an ever more fervent and telling evangelical witness by religious of the different orders and institutes in the Church and the world and gladly gives you and all participants the propitiatory apostolic blessing asked for.

Confirma Fratres Tuos
(Luke 22:32)

The invitation to address you on this occasion is a special honor for which I thank you sincerely. I come to you as a diocesan priest who has been in the ministry of service to religious for many years. The evolution of my vocation traces my first contacts with religious during the eight years I lived as a religious teaching brother. Since I have been involved in the ministry of the House of Affirmation, I have spoken with hundreds of religious in therapy, and conducted workshops with several communities in both the East and West. I sincerely feel I am in a privileged position to reflect with you during these days.

Since your secretary, Father Systermans, has asked me to speak on the House of Affirmation ministry, I desire that some of what the House of Affirmation is in particular may influence congregations in general. I come to you as a priest and pastor of souls who employs psychology and the behavioral sciences as instruments of ministry. Yet, I fully realize, and once again state clearly, that the religious life is not merely a pattern of human behavior; it is an operation of divine grace, and as such, lies beyond our understanding.

The theme of your meeting, *"Confirma Fratres Tuos,"* "Strengthen Your Brothers," is also the theme of the House of Affirmation. The word affirmation is taken from the Latin, *affirmare*, and means "to make firm," "to make strong." Allow me, please, to continue to explain how we of the House of Affirmation ministry offer strength to our brothers and sisters.

Historical Background

The House of Affirmation is an outgrowth of the Worcester Consulting Center for Clergy and Religious which was established in 1970 in response to the expressed needs of the priests and religious in the diocese, with the enthusiastic support of the Most Reverend Bernard J. Flanagan, D.D. The impact of Vatican II had been strongly felt by the clergy and religious who were meeting increased pressures from the demands of decentralization and responsible involvement in social and ecclesial issues. The services of the consulting center would provide priests and religious the opportunity for self-discovery through the contemporary approach of psychology in ongoing dialogue with theological developments.

The members of the Interim Senate for Religious approached the Vicar for Priests and Religious, Most Reverend Timothy J. Harrington, D.D., Auxiliary Bishop of the Diocese of Worcester, and informed him that a sister-psychiatrist was working at the Worcester State Hospital. They suggested she would probably help in the organization of mental health services for the religious and clergy of the area. The sister, Anna Polcino, a Medical Missionary, physician-surgeon, who had returned from West Pakistan a few years earlier, was invited to membership on the planning committee which had been brought together to think through the logistics of the enterprise. She then became the first director of what was to become the Worcester Consulting Center. I was completing my postgraduate studies at that time and became codirector of the consulting center, at the request of my bishop.

The overriding goal of the consulting center was to help the clients become fully human, consistently free persons within the context of their ecclesial calling and social insertion. Sister Anna and I undertook to meet this goal through a threefold program of service, education, and research.

After two full years of operation, however, it became apparent to us that the outpatient facilities were not sufficient for some religious and clergy who had come to the consulting center; there was definite need for an intensive residential treatment program. Thus was the House of Affirmation residential center conceived. It became a reality in October 1973, when the doors opened to its first residents in Whitinsville, Massachusetts. Sister Anna Polcino, S.C.M.M., M.D., assumed the responsibility of psychiatric director of therapy and I became the executive director. The residential center pursues the same goals as the consulting center; namely, service, education, and research.

In 1974, a Boston office of the House of Affirmation opened and is now directed by Reverend James P. Madden, C.S.C. In 1977, a second residential center was opened in Montara, California, directed by Reverend Bernard J. Bush, S.J. The third residential center was opened in Knowle, England in 1978, under the direction of Sister Fiona Vallance. In 1979, a fourth residential center was opened in Webster Groves, Missouri, with Sister Kathleen E. Kelley, S.N.D., as its director.

The variety of programs offered by the House of Affirmation includes residential psychotheological therapy, outpatient therapy, career and candidate assessment, consultation to religious communities, a formation ministry program, creative potential development courses, and a publishing division to disseminate literature of interest to priests, seminarians, and religious.

Philosophy of the House of Affirmation

The philosophy underlying the House of Affirmation's existence and operation can be succinctly stated as treatment of the whole person in a wholly therapeutic environment. Mental health professionals adhering to this basic philosophy meet a real challenge when their clientele is made up of other professionals whose religious values are central to their vocational choice and identity. Religious men and women have chosen a celibate way of life which jars with the usual Freudian model of therapy. Thus, an alternative therapeutic mode had to evolve to meet the needs of this relatively important and clearly delineated sociological group of celibate priests and religious seeking psychological help.

A group situation provides a favorable environment for the social relearning that constitutes therapy. Modern psychology emphasizes the tremendous effect of the environment on human development; our surroundings exert a molding influence on our behavior. In milieu therapy, the expectancies and attitudes of the treatment staff are central to bringing about social rehabilitation. The psychotheological community concept of the House of Affirmation goes beyond this milieu therapy with its inherent psychoanalytic orientation and reductionism. We have an existential concern with rediscovering the living person amid the compartmentalization and dehumanization of modern culture. Interest centers on reality as immediately experienced by the person with the accent on the inner, personal character of the client's experience. The therapeutic community supplies the type of accepting or impartial reactions from others that favor social learning. Furthermore, the therapeutic environment prevents further disorganization in the clients' behavior by reducing their intense anxieties.

Our treatment philosophy, as the name implies, is affirmation of the whole person. Affirmation is the positive response to the recognized goodness of the other.[1] It is an experience of a kind of relationship that is creative of the person. The opposite of affirmation is denial, or nonrecognition and nonresponse to the other. The effect of denial is psychic annihilation.[2] Nonaffirmed persons have generally experienced deprivation of affection in childhood, which is later reinforced by the impersonality and task orientation of religious life. When personal worth is unrecognized and unacknowledged by others, religious come to believe that they have no value. Nonaffirmed persons can go through the motions of a productive life and even look outwardly happy, but much of the appearance is pretense. Inside there is anxiety, fear, insecurity, feelings of

---

1. Pieper, *About Love*, p. 69.

2. Bernard J. Bush, S.J., "Healing Grace," *The Way* 16 (July 1976): 189-198.

worthlessness, and depression. Efforts to boost themselves and reassurances from others do not seem to touch the deeper core where the unrest lies. Such feelings then produce behavior which is self-defeating, such as attention seeking, physical complaints, excessive busyness, hostility masked by a cheerful facade, addictions, futile attempts to please others, conflict with peers and authorities, and compulsive sexual acting out. Such behavior serves only to increase loneliness and guilt-laden depression.

These problems are not cured by intensified spiritual practices or facile reassurances that one is okay, but by the genuine felt love of another that makes no demands. Such unqualified love creates a nonthreatening environment where persons feel secure enough simply "to be." An atmosphere of consistent affirmation gives them the necessary personal space and freedom to develop their human identity as the base on which to build religious and community identities.

Faith assures us that we can have confidence in the presence of the Holy Spirit who permeates the process. Through contemplative reflection on personal experience enlightened by the scriptural revelation of God's ways with humans, religious prophetically call attention to that presence. This witness may not even involve much God-talk. It can simply be radiation of the inner joy and richness of our life in the spirit.

Psychotheological Therapeutic Community

The House of Affirmation has developed a unique model in its psychotheological therapeutic community. The expression psychotheological community implies a quest

for communion with God and with other human beings.[3]
It is an accepted fact that personhood can only be realized
in community, and this phenomenological aspect of man's
human predicament aligns the model with the existential
therapeutic movement.[4] The community seeks to analyze
the structure of the religious' human existence in view of
understanding the reality underlying their being-in-crisis. It
is concerned with the profound dimensions of the emotional and spiritual temper of contemporary human
beings.

The importance of community looms large in the current
psychological literature. E. Mark Stern and Bert Marino
state that "religion and psychotherapy encourage community engagement with life; both can be distorted to emphasize a kind of pulling back in order to ensure personal
safety. Insofar as they foster openness, they become true
protectors of the role that love can play in cementing
human relationships, and consequently, the reconciliation
of society. The establishment of relationships is the first
step in establishing the community. As a stranger becomes
familiar, we are in a better position to reach out to him, to
join our lives more closely. Our differences will never disappear and we will find it necessary to sacrifice a degree of
autonomy."[5]

---

3. Sister Anna Polcino, S.C.M.M., M.D., "Psychotheological
Community," *The Priest* 31 (September 1975): 19.

4. Thomas A. Kane, "Psychotheological Therapy" in *New
Catholic Encyclopedia,* vol. 17 (Washington, DC: McGraw-Hill,
1979): 546-48.

5. E. Mark Stern and Bert G. Marino, *Psychotheology*
(Paramus, NY: Newman Press, 1970), p. 65.

Unique Identity of Individual

Each person in the community remains unique. Individuals may grow and change in the community but they will retain their identity. Personal union of community members serves to bring out and enrich what is uniquely true of each individual. Growth in community will be effected by all those active and passive elements that create favorable conditions for the growth of unity and charity: openness, receptivity, sharing, giving, receiving. Community connotes oneness without loss of identity, a sharing in the interiority of another without the sacrifice of personal integrity.

The adaptations recommended and wrought by the Second Vatican Council have changed the pattern of environmental demands on Christians at large, but they have wrought this change even more on formally professed religious men and women. Some have adjusted quickly and almost eagerly to these changes while others have been floundering in the insecurity of a slow and painful assimilation of change. The poignant experience of confusion, doubt, and sense of loss has taxed the coping ability of many religious who, cut off from safe moorings, question their identity and authenticity on what they consider an uncharted sea. The post-Vatican period demands maturity and balance on the part of those individuals chosen to minister to the people of God, especially because much risk is involved.

The Dogmatic Constitution on the Church, *Lumen Gentium*, emphasized the element of community when it spoke of the Church as a "sign and sacrament of man's union with God and of the unity of the whole human race" (LG, 1). The religious community as such cannot form the person although it should provide a setting in which the individual human being can emerge as a fully functioning adult. For too long, religious communities of men and women have had a task-oriented rather than person-oriented environment. Yet personal development is a basic prerequisite to a meaningful life in society at large and in the local community where the celibate lives. This follows logically from the principle that love of self precedes love of others. However, I can only know myself if another reveals me to myself just as I can only come to a real love of self when I come to the realization that I am affirmed by another.[6] So do we all find our meaning and sense of identity in and through others. The person-oriented group helps us realize our personhood when, through the truth and goodness of our companions, our own powers of knowing and loving are released.

Social Interaction

In the therapeutic community of the House of Affirmation, the residents can formulate their own reactions, share them in social communication, and thus become aware of the commonness of their own anxieties. By sharing their reactions with peers, they are practicing the very techniques of social interaction in which they have typically remained unskilled. In the reactions of their peers with whom they share their daily activities, the residents find the acceptance, support, protection, and challenge which enable them to develop more valid self-reactions. In addition, the therapeutic milieu provides the opportunity for social interaction among residents and staff.

---

6. Kane, *The Healing Touch of Affirmation,* p. 41.

The House of Affirmation is neither a place of confinement nor a haven for rest and recreation; rather, it is a miniature social-religious community planned and controlled to facilitate the social learning of its residents. The professional staff members have accepted as the general goal of psychotherapy to help the "unfree," childishly dependent person become a genuine adult capable of "responding affirmatively to life, people and society."[7] The focus is on self-understanding and insight building of an immediate and current nature in view of helping individuals to grasp the meaning of their existence in its historical totality. Ultimately, the mentally healthy client will attain freedom to choose, maturity in outlook, and responsible independence.

The lives of celibates can be viewed as an ongoing process of interaction with the religious, social, and natural forces that make up their environment. The meaning that life assumes for a celibate depends on the individual's personal response to these forces. The celibate community constitutes a union of persons who participate in a common love response to the call of Christ.[8]

Participation in Community

The key to a proper understanding of community lies in participation which becomes a unifying force that, at the same time, allows for individual differences. Is not willingness to receive from another one of the dearest gifts I can

---

7. John Dalrymple, *The Christian Affirmation* (Denville, NJ: Dimension Books, 1971), p. 10.

8. Sister Helen Marie Beha, OSF, *Living Community* (Milwaukee, WI: Bruce Publishing, 1967), p. 21.

give to that person? Participation characterizes the relationship of individuals united by love in community. All encounters assume meaning in that context; they become avenues to change.

The difference their presence makes in the overall community process gives meaning to the celibates' lives. Being human really means coming to grips, in a creative way, with the concrete situation in which they find themselves. The experience of here-and-now is crucial, for life is today—not yesterday or tomorrow. The same truth applies in the therapeutic situation, be it individual or group: the ongoing, immediate experience of residents and therapists as they interact becomes the phenomenological focus in therapy. The total phenomena experienced at any moment in time is what describes the human existential situation; the experienced event is what is brought to therapy. Listening to others as persons, looking into their eyes, minds, and hearts with deep sympathy, feeling that this person is suffering, is appealing to us as a person: is this not our affirmative response to Christ's summons, "Love one another as I have loved you" (John 13:34)?

Community of Faith

The call to Christian life is ideally expressed in the Eucharistic experience which is the community experience par excellence. The Eucharist builds up a community of faith, and so it stands at the very center of the psycho-theological community that is the House of Affirmation; it reveals the solidarity of all members in Christ. This same solidarity is expressed in the opening words of the Pastoral Constitution on the Church in the Modern World,

Gaudium et Spes: "The joys and hopes, the sorrows and worries of the men of our time are ours" (GS, 1). The House of Affirmation has thus accepted the challenge of the Fathers of Vatican II who urge in the same document that we make appropriate use "not only of theological principles, but also of the findings of the secular sciences, especially of psychology and sociology" (GS, 62) to help the faithful live their faith in a more thorough and mature way. In the Decree on the Appropriate Renewal of the Religious Life, *Perfectae Caritatis*, the Council Fathers pursued the same line of thought: "The manner of living, praying, and working should be suitably adapted to the physical and psychological conditions of today's religious, . . . to the needs of the apostolate, the requirements of a given culture, and to the social and economic circumstances" (PC, 3). In the article pertaining to chastity, religious are urged to "take advantage of those natural helps which favor mental and bodily health. . . . Everyone should remember that chastity has stronger safeguards in a community when true fraternal love thrives among its members" (PC, 12). Celibate religious who are trained in psychiatry and psychology can use their own experience in coming to a better understanding of the emotional problems of religious and priestly life today. Such is the case in the centers of the House of Affirmation.

For too long, celibates have been frustrated when seeking professional help because they were limited to psychiatrists and psychologists who had little understanding of the religious commitment. The misconceptions that could arise often deterred religious and priests from seeking psychiatric-psychological help. Our residential treatment centers have been set up to minimize the threat and the possible alienation attendant on presenting oneself to an institutional-type establishment. A homelike atmosphere has been developed which has proved most therapeutic and which prepares the individual to respond to therapy in a very positive manner, strongly contrasting with the resistance that is frequently found when working with the laity.

Willingness is Crucial

Individual priests, sisters, brothers, deacons, or seminarians may be referred to the House of Affirmation for the purpose of coming to a better understanding of their emotional problems and working to resolve them. However, clients are always informed that unless they come of their own free will, therapy will avail them little. No residents are accepted for treatment merely on the recommendation of their religious superiors; the applicants must indicate willingness to come for therapy. The principle of confidentiality is crucial to the operation of the House of Affirmation; privacy is maintained at all times. This policy has produced a sense of security and trust, and the clientele has grown geometrically. Since its inception, the House of Affirmation has stressed that its purpose is not so much keeping celibates in the religious or priestly life as helping them to become truly human and consistently free. Through therapy, they can come to their own decision about their future.

In the course of therapy, clients come to view their experiences in a wider perspective and they gain a better future orientation. Self-growth demands that individuals have something to aim for, a goal which can be realized through committed action. Their task will then be to actualize this possibility, to make it a reality. As they begin to respond to their feelings, they see possibilities in their future and attempt to realize them. By so doing, they increase responsible independence in their lifestyle.

Deprivation Syndromes

Many of the problems presented to us at the House of Affirmation have been classified as deprivation syndromes or as what contemporary psychological science describes as repressive neurosis. In the first case, lack of love and acceptance (lack of affirmation) has crippled the psychological functioning of individuals; in the latter case, one encounters priests and religious who have made excessive use of the defense mechanism known as intellectualization. Many of these individuals are not aware of their emotions and have even repressed anger in their celibate lives. In this instance the repression often came about through faulty training which presented the emotion of anger as "unvirtuous," an emotion not to be expressed at any time. Yet Christ found it appropriate to express his emotions: "The angry man who picked up a cord to drive the buyers and sellers out of the temple, who wept in sadness over Jerusalem, who was bathed in sweat before his arrest was not a stoical, emotionless man."[9]

Through therapy, individual clients become aware of their emotions, are informed that their emotions are basically good, and are encouraged to express these emotions in a healthy way within the context of a celibate life. Individual therapy is supported by group therapy where feelings of anger can be expressed and accepted. The reeducative process is somewhat long and painful, but it

---

9. Dalrymple, *Christian Affirmation*, p. 111.

results in a more personally satisfying and productive life. Having been affirmed by significant others in the course of individual therapy and, in turn, having affirmed others, the healed residents know and feel who they are. They find that they are different from others but that they are acceptable, that they belong in community, that they are contributing to it and changing it. They have come to realize that there is a unique place for them in society, that they have a unique contribution to make to it, and that they can choose freely to do and to love.[10]

To Heal and be Healed

To rediscover the life springs within, a therapeutic community such as the House of Affirmation, and by extension, every religious community, should be a place where truth, reality, and faith prevail.[11] The grace of healing is present in the community as a whole and in the individuals of that community. The same grace is given to the one who is healing and to the one who is being healed. All are called upon both to be healed and to be healers of others, no matter how much one may be personally hurting. It is my conviction that the grace of healing is given precisely at the growing edge of the personality. A person is healed when most exposed and vulnerable, and likewise performs the most graceful healing when the sore places are reaching out tenderly to touch another. When facade relates to facade, or even when facade relates to suffering humanity, there is only a pretense of loving and caring. The head may be

---

10. Kane, *Who Controls Me?*, pp. 75-76.

11. Bernard J. Bush, S.J., *Living In His Love* (Whitinsville, MA: Affirmation Books, 1978), pp. 107-15.

present to the other, but the heart is not. The grace of healing is mediated through the humanity of each person in the community.

In our special healing community, the House of Affirmation, the principal responsibility for creating the atmosphere, developing programs, and so forth, lies with the staff. Each of us has come to this work through a personal odyssey of suffering, healing, change, and growth. We are willing to share our weakness, and it is our greatest strength. We are constantly being reminded of our own frailty and limitations. Yet, just as constantly, we discover the unfolding mystery of the action of God in our lives. This confidence in the strength and love of God gives us the willingness to risk feelings and responses of genuine love to the goodness of the other which is more important for healing than clinical skill alone. However, without the clinical expertise, we could easily lose our way in the problems that present themselves. Our task is to be both loving and professional.

Intellectualization

We have found that in most religious, intellectual and sometimes spiritual growth has outstripped emotional development. The characteristic defense mechanism of religious is intellectualization, in which feared emotional responses are cut off from and repressed by the intellect. Eventually the person becomes unable to feel anything at all. In our therapeutic program, the religious can discover and actualize creative potentialities through guided trial and error, and incorporate them into the whole process of growth. Thus, individuals come to understand the uniqueness of their own learning style and pace of growth. Nothing is forced or unnatural.

Another important dimension of our life together is the opportunity for men and women to live in the same community, and to learn to relate to one another as persons rather than as objects of fear or fantasy. This kind of living sometimes gives rise to reactions that are characteristic of delayed adolescence. When such feelings arise, they become the material for guided growth toward sexual maturity within the context of celibacy and its limits. We have found that celibacy as such is not the main problem of most clients who come to us. Rather, their lack of affirmation and affection leads to problems in the area of sexuality. Only a small proportion of those who have come through our program have left religious life.

Prayerful Therapeutic Process

We firmly believe that our therapy is a work of collaboration with the healing spirit of God in humanity. This work demands much reflection and contemplation of where and how God is present with his healing grace in each person. In this prayerful therapeutic process, the neurotic barriers to inner freedom in both the healer and healed are discovered, exposed, and removed. Growth in freedom and the consequent acceptance of increased responsibility demand deep faith in the Incarnation, that God is among us in human flesh.[12] Our goal, then, is to

---

12. Sister Philomena Agudo, F.M.M., *Affirming the Human and the Holy* (Whitinsville, MA: Affirmation Books, 1979), pp. 45-53.

help religious with emotional disorders to achieve a balanced and integrated personhood, wherein all feelings are joyfully accepted and guided by the graced and gentle light of reason and will. To achieve this goal we have provided a milieu where the process of conversion from denial to affirmation can be experienced. Our clients are becoming healed and are returning to creative service in the Church. The House files contain many letters from former residents and nonresidents testifying to the permanence of the growth and changes that have occurred in their lives. The sad part is that frequently their communities and work situations have not changed. At the end of the course of treatment there is a renewed sense of the loving presence of God at deeper levels of the personality and in increased desire for prayer. It is not uncommon for persons prior to discharge to make a directed retreat with an affective responsiveness that was simply impossible before coming to us.

Observations

I would like, finally, to make some observations about preventive mental health in religious community life:

1. There is still among us a strong strain of moralism and idealistic perfectionism which compounds depressive guilt feelings and compulsive self-destructive behavior. We find that many of the neuroses we treat are aggravated by styles of spirituality and community life that encourage religious to be slavishly dependent, to intellectualize and mask the so-called negative feelings, and to try to be happy without giving and receiving genuine affection and warm love.

2. There is also a tendency to consume too much valuable energy with introspective community reorganization and constant revamping of structures. This inward-looking tendency stifles the apostolic spirit of reaching out to others in their need. Meetings upon meetings can have a very depressing effect on people. This is not to negate, however, the need for congregations to learn from contemporary sciences the nature and meaning of effective communication techniques.

3. Religious particularly need to be reminded that they need to say no and set limits on the demands that others make on their time and energy. A fine balance must be struck between helping others and being good to oneself. This means that religious and priests need to find outlets for creative recreation and hobbies, and to develop the ability to have fun and "waste time" enjoyably in ways that are enriching.

4. Leisure time should be allowed for the development of friendships with persons of one's own choice, whether of the same or the other sex. Relationships in all their aspects are at the center of many of the problems in religious congregations today. Healthy appreciation of relationships with Christ and neighbor assures the continuity and fruitfulness of the religious life.

5. For healthy living, time should also be set aside for contemplative reflection on one's own emotional and spiritual life in order fully to enjoy being alive and feeling. Prayer is time spent with the Lord, fostering an affective relationship with him. In an

atmosphere of loving trust, I can bring my other affective relationships to the Lord, so that they can develop under the guidance of his spirit without fear of reprisal or condemnation, since they also are God-given.

6. To be a sign to the world, religious life must have something of that counterculture that was the challenge of Jesus to his world. This fact has implications in the areas of justice and the use of power, and also in the area of functionalism. Many religious are so busy working for the apostolate in the name of the Good Shepherd that if he were to walk into the room they would be too busy doing "holy work" even to see or recognize him. Yet the religious bears witness to Jesus, and we must give priority of time to community and individual prayer and meditation.

7. A community goal should be for each member to strive to discover and encourage every aspect of the others' total life situation that is truly life giving and affirming. Community members should be able to feel themselves as both healers and as needing to be healed by others.

8. We need honest and frank conversation in community without censuring or judging. There must be freedom to confront and challenge lovingly, in order to prevent an irresponsible permissiveness.

9. Congregations can become affirming when the persons in them feel that they are secure to be themselves, to make mistakes, and to find gentle forgiveness and deeply caring support one for the other. Our Church professes and proclaims that its root

and corner stone is incarnate love. Yet ironically, many religious suffer because there is a devastating lack of love in their lives.

10. Candidates for the religious life should be carefully reviewed before they enter. Psychological testing alone is insufficient. Initial and ongoing formation programs conducted by properly trained directors with the ability to affirm are essential.

In conclusion, I would like to state with gratitude that the work of the House of Affirmation has been abundantly blessed by God in the few years of its existence. We have come upon many shoals which have nearly destroyed us. In each case we have been rescued by a presence that can only be called divine. Hence we rejoice and have great hope that our efforts will continue to be blessed, and that our service and experience will make a significant contribution to enhance the life of the whole Church.

Prayer for
The House of Affirmation

O Lord Jesus Christ,

You blessed homes with Your presence and Your power;

You used to go apart to a peaceful place for quiet

and for prayer—

Through the intercession of Saint Therese,

bless the House of Affirmation,

all who seek and serve You here,

and all our friends.

Be compassionate toward those who do not

wish us well.

This we ask, in confidence, of You

who live and reign forever.

Amen